Trafficked Girl

Trafficked Girl

Zoe Patterson
and Jane Smith

Certain details in this story, including names, places and dates, have been changed to protect the family's privacy.

HarperElement
An imprint of HarperCollins*Publishers*
1 London Bridge Street
London SE1 9GF

www.harpercollins.co.uk

First published by HarperElement 2018

18 19 20 21 22 LSC 10 9 8 7 6 5 4 3 2 1

A catalogue record of this book is
available from the British Library

Extract on page 95 © Trey Parker; extract on page 293 from
Broken Vessels, Andre Dubus, David R. Godine, 1991.

ISBN 978-0-00-814804-1

Printed and bound in the United States of
America by LSC Communications

For more information visit: www.harpercollins.co.uk/green

Care: (1) the provision of what is necessary for the health, welfare, maintenance, and protection of someone or something; (2) serious attention or consideration applied to doing something correctly or to avoid damage or risk.

always wanted to live – the sort of life my mum always said I didn't deserve.

As things turned out, however, I was one of the unlucky ones for whom the care part of 'being taken into care' didn't match any dictionary definition. In fact, what happened to me while I was living at Denver House was even worse than anything that had happened to me at home. Which made me think that maybe Mum had been right all along and I really was living the life I deserved.

Prologue

For many years, I believed that what happened to me when I was a little girl was my fault. I suppose if you tell someone almost anything over and over again from a very young age, they'll grow up with it hardwired into their brain as a 'fact'. Later, when they're old enough to think for themselves, and if the fact has an objective or scientific basis, they might be able to disprove it. But that isn't so easy to do if it's something more subjective, particularly if it subsequently seems to be confirmed by other people and by apparently unconnected events.

The 'fact' I was told by my mother throughout my childhood and into adulthood was that I was to blame for all the horrible things that were done to me – many of which she actually did herself. So I was glad, although very scared, when the day came that I was taken into care. Maybe now, I thought, the bad stuff will stop happening, and then one day I'll be able to live the sort of life I've

Chapter 1

I had just woken up and was crossing the narrow landing at the top of the stairs when Mum came out of her bedroom. For some children, home is the only place they feel safe. For others, it's the one place they know they aren't. So when Mum took a step towards me, I felt the muscles in my body tense as I instinctively leaned away from her.

I was four years old, and I'd known since I was old enough to understand anything that I didn't have to have done something wrong – or, at least, nothing I was aware of – for my mum to be angry with me. On this particular morning, however, instead of shouting at me and slapping me or pulling my hair, she just stood in the doorway of her bedroom and smiled.

It wasn't a nice smile, the way I'd seen other mums smile at their kids when they came to pick them up from school. It was more like a nasty sneer, as if she knew something bad that I didn't know and was relishing the prospect of telling me what it was. She didn't say anything though, as I hovered on the landing, trying to decide whether my own anxious, tentative smile would annoy or appease her. She waited for me to take two hesitant steps down the stairs and then she pushed me.

'Oh dear, grab the handrail,' Mum called. But the concern in her voice was exaggerated and insincere, and she laughed out loud when I stumbled and fell, smacking my head into the wall at the bottom of the stairs.

I was still lying on the worn carpet in the hallway, shocked and disorientated, when Dad ran out of the living room and crouched down beside me.

'Jesus Christ, Maggie,' he shouted at Mum, who was standing smirking halfway down the stairs. 'What happened? And what's so funny? She's hurt herself.'

'Well, don't blame *me*.' Mum put her hands on her hips and glared angrily at us both. 'It's not *my* fault she's clumsy and stupid. She tripped.'

For a moment I was forgotten as they shouted and swore at each other. So I sat up, touched the painful bump on the side of my head very gently with my fingertips, then examined the red mark on my elbow that I knew would soon develop into a bruise. It felt as though someone was pounding on the inside of my skull with something very heavy, and as the sound of my parents' angry voices filled the air above me, I could feel tears stinging my eyes. But I was determined not to cry.

'What happened, Zo?' Dad put his hands under my arms and lifted me to my feet.

'I told you, she tripped. Didn't you?' Mum was smiling the nasty smile again, although less broadly this time, maybe because she didn't want Dad to see it as he guided me into the living room, where he sat me down in her chair saying, 'I'll get you some juice. That'll make you feel better.'

It was rare for anyone to be kind to me at home, and although the memory of it makes me sad when I think about it today, I was too scared at the time to appreciate Dad's concern for me, because I knew that as soon as he'd gone to work, Mum would find a way of making me pay for his attention.

I think Dad knew about some of the things she did to me, which was why he sometimes got angry with her, like he did that day. He certainly wasn't aware of all of them though, as she was careful to hide her treatment of me, particularly when I was very young, and I didn't ever say anything because I knew that if I did, my parents would shout and maybe fight with each other for a while, then Dad would go out and I'd be left alone with Mum.

So that time when she pushed me down the stairs is one of only very few occasions I can remember when Dad stood up for me. And although he did sometimes say nice things to me when I was a little girl, Mum always seemed to be standing behind him whenever he did, looking at me over his shoulder with a spiteful expression on her face that said quite clearly, 'Just you wait until he's gone to work.'

Some of the very few good memories I have of my early childhood are of standing at the front door waving to my dad as he left the house in the mornings. The happy feeling was always short-lived, however, and it would disappear as soon as the door closed, because I knew that, for the next few hours, it would just be Mum and me.

I loved both my parents when I was a little girl. Although my mum treated me very badly and I was afraid of her, I thought it was my fault she didn't seem to love me and I desperately wanted her affection. With my dad it was different, and despite the fact that he very rarely actually did anything nice for me, he sometimes stood up for me, didn't hit me and wasn't nasty to me the way Mum was. So I really did love him, in the years before I learned to be frightened of him too.

I can't recall one single instance of Mum ever being nice to me. She had only two sides to her when it came to her dealings with me – stern or nasty – and she could be very violent. In fact, the only time she ever touched me when I was a little girl was when she was pulling my hair or slapping, pinching, punching or kicking me, beating me with her fists or hitting me with the heel of her shoe, a book or, on one occasion, a baking tray. She didn't ever hug me, or put her hands on me for any other reason except in anger. And it seemed that she was always angry with me, however hard I tried not to do anything that might irritate or antagonise her. It wasn't until much later that I realised I didn't really *do* anything to justify her cruel mind-games and vicious physical attacks. To my mum, I was simply a scapegoat, someone to blame for all the problems she had, many of which must have resulted from her own damaging childhood, although I didn't find out about that until much later, when it was almost too late for me to be able to understand and accept the truth, which was that I had never really been the problem at all.

She would sometimes throw things at Dad too, or smash ornaments when they were fighting. But she never did to him – or to my brothers – any of the vicious things she did to me, I suppose for the same reason most bullies don't pick fights with people who can fight back.

Fortunately, when I was alone in the house with her before I started going to nursery, when Dad was at work and my older brothers were at school, she spent almost all day every day in the kitchen. I don't know whether she was already drinking at that time, but I think she probably was. So maybe that's what she was doing in there while I was in the living room, trapped at a distance from her by the baby gate that blocked the doorway.

It was during that period of my childhood that Mum started refusing me access to the potty, and later to the toilet. I don't know if she did it out of spite, to humiliate me, or if it was simply another way of exercising control over me. The baby gate was just a piece of wood my granddad had cut to size and attached across the doorway, but I wasn't allowed to touch it, and never tried to again after the first time, when Mum beat me and shouted at me. So when I needed to use the potty, I would stand close to it and cry, while Mum either ignored me or watched me from the kitchen, impassively at first, then with increasing amusement when my discomfort turned to pain as I tried to hold it in. Then, when I soiled myself, as I always inevitably did, she would shout in my face and hit me, which made me believe that it really was my fault, however long she'd made me wait.

Sometimes, when I was a bit older and the baby gate had been removed, she would leave a tin plate in the middle of the kitchen floor for me to use as a toilet, as though I was a dog or a cat rather than a human child. I was probably four when she started doing it, and perfectly able to use the potty or go to the toilet by myself, but it was difficult doing it on a plate, particularly when she was watching me, as she often did, and I knew that if I misjudged it and let even the smallest drop spill over on to the floor, she would hit me.

Dad did shifts in a factory at that time and when he was working at night she'd quite often drink herself into a stupor, then fall asleep on the sofa. My brothers, Jake and Ben, who are nine and seven years older than me respectively, were old enough to put themselves to bed by the time I was born. But between the ages of three and five, I was often left downstairs on those nights and although I suppose I must have got *some* sleep, I don't know when or where. I just remember wandering around the house in the dark, then seeing the sun shining in through a window and knowing that it was morning again. Mum would always make me get dressed quickly on those mornings, before my brothers woke up, and as she pulled my hair and hit me with her hairbrush she would warn me, 'Don't you dare tell Ben or Jake, or your dad, that you haven't been to bed.'

I suppose those sleepless nights were the reason why I often fell asleep during the day when I started nursery school, and later in the reception class at primary school. In fact, I can remember on one occasion waking up in a state of near-panic when my teacher threw her shoe at me, then told me off for sleeping in class.

Mum did sometimes carry me up to bed when I'd fallen asleep. And sometimes she would drop me, then shout at me as I was tumbling down the stairs, 'That was *your* fault,' before stamping down to where I was lying in a crumpled heap, grabbing me by the arm and dragging me up to my bedroom, where she would almost throw me on to my bed. And on those occasions too, I would be determined not to cry, although I came very close to it whenever she said, in a spooky, sneering voice, 'Watch out for wandering hands in your bed tonight.' Then I would hear her laughing as she closed the door, shutting out all the light as she stomped back down the stairs.

I wasn't allowed to get out of bed for any reason without Mum's permission. So when I woke up from a nightmare, as I often did, I sometimes wet myself. The first time it happened, I cried and screamed for my mum, but no one came. So I lay for the rest of the night on the wet mattress and waited fearfully for the morning. She must have heard me whenever I called out in the night because she always seemed to know when she came into my room the next morning that the mattress would be wet, and after she'd yanked me out of bed, she'd drag me around the room by my hair, slapping me and shouting that I was worthless and stupid and did nothing but cause trouble for everyone. Then she would strip the wet sheet off my bed, take it downstairs and show it to my brothers, who would laugh with her and make fun of me.

We had a washing machine, so it wasn't a huge deal having to wash a wet sheet, although perhaps it seemed like it to her, because when I finally stopped wetting the bed at the age of seven, she only ever washed my bedding once a year.

Mum never took me anywhere and she'd be angry on the rare occasions that Dad ever did, like the day when he got home after working the night shift and decided to take me with him to the supermarket. I think I was four years old, and I don't know if I'd asked to go, or why Mum kept insisting on him leaving me at home. But the more she argued with him, the more determined he became, until eventually he shouted, 'I'm taking her,' then pushed me ahead of him out of the house before slamming the front door behind him.

Maybe their argument would have ended there if I hadn't fallen asleep on the bus on the way back from the supermarket, and if Dad hadn't told Mum it was her fault I was so tired and accused her – with more justification than I think he realised at the time – of not looking after me properly. So then they had a huge fight, while I tried to shut out the sound of their angry, hate-filled voices and not see what they were doing to each other.

I don't think Mum's reaction was because she was jealous. I think she just didn't want me to have any positive experiences at all. And in the end she got her way, as she almost always did.

The only place Mum ever took me – and then only on very rare occasions – was to the supermarket. I certainly didn't ever go to a cinema, a bowling alley or a park with her, and although my brothers had regular check-ups at the dentist, I never did. Even when I needed a haircut or new school uniform, it was my brother Ben who took me into town and paid for it with money Dad would give him. In fact, I only ever went to a playground once when I was a child.

It was on another occasion when Dad had taken me with him to the supermarket and we were on the way back that he said, 'Come on, Zoe. Let's go to the park.' It was only a five-minute walk from our house, but although he'd been there many times with Jake and Ben when they were young, he'd never taken me. So I was very excited, and because I didn't want him to change his mind, I didn't ask him the question I was asking myself, which was, 'What will Mum say if she finds out?'

When we got to the park, Dad took a white hankie out of his pocket and laid it carefully on the seat of the swing – 'So that you don't get your clothes dirty,' he told me, which made me feel very special, like a princess. Then he pushed me, gently at first, until I got more confident and started shouting, 'Higher! Higher!'

As all princesses know, however, there's a wicked witch in every fairy tale and ours was waiting for us when we got home. Dad had only just opened the front door when she started shouting at him, asking what took us so long and demanding to know where we'd been. 'We went to the fucking park,' he told her, just before she hit him. Then he hit her and the row quickly escalated into a full-blown physical fight.

Whereas Dad had to be sober for at least a few hours every day when he was working at the factory, Mum had no such constraint and was eventually drinking more or less from the moment she woke up in the morning until the moment she fell asleep at night. And the more they both drank, the more frequent and violent their arguments became. So I spent many hours of my childhood listening to them shouting and hitting each other, and hearing Mum scream, 'No! Stop it!' when Dad lay on top of her and did something that made her struggle as she tried to push him off, which made *me* feel protective towards her, and guilty because I knew I couldn't do anything to make him stop.

Looking back on it now, I'm glad Dad took me to the park that day, because although it ended in him and Mum having a horrible fight, he didn't ever take me again. So at least I have that good memory of him pushing me on a swing before his attitude towards me began to change and it stopped being just Mum's beatings that made me afraid to be in my own home.

Chapter 2

Jake and Ben used to bully me a lot when I was a child. But whereas Ben was sometimes nice to me, Jake never was, and he would often beat me and call me names like bitch, slag and slut, which I was too young to understand. I think he probably would have treated me the same way even if he hadn't been encouraged by the fact that whenever Mum heard him tormenting me, she would laugh and join in, calling me 'thunder thighs' or saying I was ugly and fat, or that I had a hideous smile and a pig's nose. I was just four years old when she bought me a pair of pig slippers – 'Because they look just like you.'

The fact that Jake was nine and Ben was seven when I was born meant that by the time I was old enough to do anything, they were already leading their own lives and I had very little contact with either of them during my childhood, particularly with Jake. But although Mum was almost always angry with me, she rarely was with my brothers. So I believed her when she said there was something wrong with me and that I was the cause of all the rows and everything else that was stressful in her life. Everyone else did too, particularly when they saw how differently she treated my brothers, who were included as an integral part of the family and given pretty much free rein to do whatever they wanted whenever they wanted. What other explanation could there be of why a mother would love two of her children and so vehemently hate the other one?

Then, not long before I was due to start school, Mum had another baby.

I sometimes wonder what would have happened if my little brother Michael had been a girl – whether Mum would have hated her the way she hated me, or whether a little sister would have been included in the family the way Michael was when he was born. I often wonder if the physical contact I had with him when Mum wasn't well and I used to have to give him his bottle was what made me able to identify and empathise with other people later, when I grew up, because he was the only human being I ever cuddled and hugged.

Mum had more or less recovered from her illness by the time I started school, so I was glad to have somewhere to escape to. I hadn't ever played with other children before going to nursery – my older brothers only ever teased or bullied me – but despite having no experience of socialising, I got on well with the other kids and really enjoyed school, for the first few years at least, until what was happening at home made it difficult for me to cope with anything.

Despite being abused and excluded by my family, I accepted everything that happened at home as being normal. I think I was about ten years old by the time I even thought to compare my life and my brothers' with any sense that the difference might be unfair. It was just the way things were: my brothers sat in the living room watching television and eating their meals with our parents, while I sat alone in my bedroom.

I spent many, many hours of my childhood on my own, sitting on the floor in the middle of my room staring at the walls. I wasn't allowed to sit on the bed, move the furniture or play with any of the toys Mum arranged strategically on a shelf so that she'd know if I'd touched anything. I wasn't even allowed to open the wardrobe or drawers until I was at least 11. Mum used to give me some clothes every morning and say, 'This is what you're wearing today.' It was all about control, although obviously I didn't realise that at the time. All I knew was that if I got so bored of just sitting there doing nothing that I managed to convince myself I'd be able to put something back exactly as I'd found it, she always knew. Then she'd shout at me and beat me, often with a half-smile on her face that reflected the enjoyment I think she got from punishing me.

There must have been many reasons for Mum's behaviour, some of which I partially understand now, and some of which will, I'm sure, be locked away forever in the murky depths of her own psyche. One thing I did eventually become aware of is that she has obsessive-compulsive disorder, which got worse over the years, but which was already apparent in many of the things she did when I was a small child – although again, I didn't realise that at the time. Some indications of it included the way she used to line things up on the bathroom windowsill – bottles and plastic containers of make-up all placed just so, and woe betide anyone who moved them – and the fact that, later, she always chose a cake bar and crisps to put in my school lunchbox that had a colour-matched wrapper and packet, which I used to think was an indication of the fact that she did care about me after all. Even today, she puts what she calls 'traps' around her house – an ornament or rug positioned at a particular angle, for example, or little stones lined up by her wheelie bin so that she'll know if anyone has moved it, although I'm not sure why anyone would.

Not allowing me to sit on the bed after she'd made it, move anything or play with the few toys I had in my bedroom might have been aspects of OCD, if it hadn't been for the fact that there were no such restrictions on my brothers. So I do think it was more of a control thing with me.

Usually, she would bring meals up to my room and I'd eat them there on my own, isolated from the rest of the family. I used to sit on the floor in my bedroom for hours, anxiously watching the door, waiting for it to burst open and for Mum to accuse me of doing something wrong, even when I wasn't doing anything at all. I would sit on the floor in the living room too, on the rare occasions when I was allowed downstairs to watch television with the rest of my family. Sometimes, I'd hide behind the sofa, hoping they'd forget I was there, because I didn't ever know why or when Mum might launch an attack on me.

In view of the way I was alienated and excluded from the family by my mum at every opportunity, it might seem odd to say that I've always had a strong sense of who I am, in some respects at least. The first time I think I ever became consciously aware of 'me' was when I was four years old and at nursery school. It was a very hot day and I was pushing a little lad around the playground on a toy tractor when he started pulling off his T-shirt. It seemed an obvious thing to do once he'd done it. So I took mine off too, and was startled when I realised a few seconds later that it was *me* the teacher was shouting at.

I can still remember how indignant I felt. Why was she picking on me, telling me to put my T-shirt on but not saying anything to the little boy? How was that fair? Although I'd learned not to expect fairness from my mum – and wouldn't have dreamed of defying *her* in the same situation – I must have expected it from my teacher, because instead of doing as she told me, I bent down again and was just about to continue pushing the tractor when I saw her grab my T-shirt and start striding purposefully across the playground towards me. I don't know what the reason was for my uncharacteristic defiance, but before she was halfway across the playground, I had taken to my heels.

Just a few days earlier, I'd watched an old black-and-white film with my brothers in which a man who was being chased slipped into the space between two buildings and his pursuer ran straight past. Although I was beyond the stage of covering my eyes with my hands and thinking no one could see me, I hadn't quite understood how the incident in the film worked. So, as I was circling the nursery playground with my teacher in hot pursuit, I suddenly darted down the side of the building, flattened myself against the hot bricks and waited for her to run past. Then, a minute or two later, I resumed my game with the little boy, wearing my T-shirt and seething with righteous indignation.

It was an insignificant incident in itself, but I've held on to it – and a few similar memories – all these years because sometimes, when I seem to be in danger of forgetting, it reminds me who I am.

I don't know what my dad was like before he married Mum. Maybe he was a completely different person and just got worn down by her until he began to accept her dysfunctional behaviour as normal. He was several years older than Mum and had been married and widowed for about ten years before they met. I think his first wife died suddenly and unexpectedly in her early twenties, by which time they already had a little boy, who went to live with

Dad's mum, apparently because that's what his wife requested when she found out she was going to die.

Perhaps the reason Dad didn't look after the little boy himself was because he wasn't a very reliable parent even before he met my mum. Or maybe his wife knew he would fall apart when she died, because I know he found it really difficult trying to deal with her death and was still working long hours so that he didn't have to face it ten years later, when he met Mum. Perhaps that also explained why he made what turned out to be the huge mistake of ignoring the warning 'marry in haste, repent at leisure' and married her just two weeks later. She was still living with her parents at the time, so for her it was a means of escaping, which I now know she had good reason to want to do.

I don't know how often Dad saw his first son, Ian, after he and Mum got married, but she more or less put a stop to any contact they did have when Jake was born – and with the rest of his family too, who we rarely saw when I was growing up.

Dad used to love singing karaoke at the pub and one day he came home with a karaoke machine he'd bought for a few pounds when they were throwing it out. Mum just sat there scowling when he took it into the living room and plugged it in, and after he'd sung a couple of songs himself, he told me to sing some of the nursery rhymes I'd just learnt at nursery school. 'I'm going to record them,' he said. 'Then, when you're an old lady, you can listen to them and remember what you used to sound like when you were four.'

I was too young to understand the concept of one day being old, like my nan. But I can remember feeling really pleased when Dad said I had a nice voice, then laughed and added, 'You must have inherited it from me,' which made Mum scowl even more.

The only other happy childhood memory I have is of another day when I was four and Dad took me to a big garden that was open to the public, where there was a lake and a real elephant that he paid for me to sit on and have my photograph taken. I can still remember how rough the elephant's skin felt where it touched my bare legs.

Maybe Dad did other things with me on other days as well, but I can't remember any of them now. I just remember that I loved him and that although he didn't often do anything positive to make my life better, he wasn't ever violent or mean to me when I was a little girl.

My nan was though – mean rather than violent – and I knew from a very young age that she didn't like me. She and Granddad didn't come to our house very often, but one day when they were there – I think it was around Christmastime when I was five – I asked Granddad to go upstairs with me because I wanted to show him something in my bedroom and Nan gave me a really cold look, then insisted on coming too.

When we got up to my room, they both sat on the bed while I looked for whatever it was I wanted to show him.

I wasn't used to having an audience and I was chattering away excitedly when I noticed that Granddad was staring at me in a peculiar way. Glancing quickly at my nan for reassurance, I realised she was scowling at me, for some reason I couldn't understand. I'd had a lot of practice reading my mum's facial expressions by the time I was five – trying to guess how angry she was with me and what she might be going to do next – but I didn't have any idea why Nan was cross with me. So I just burbled away inanely, hoping to deflect her disapproval and not knowing why I felt so uncomfortable. Then, after a few minutes, she got up, stared at Granddad until he did the same, and we all trooped back down the stairs.

I did sometimes go to my grandparents' house after that, but I wasn't ever left there on my own again, until Granddad died when I was ten.

Maybe what I'd wanted to show my granddad that day was a new toy that had been sent to me as a Christmas present by one of Dad's sisters. Mum and Dad used to give us a few presents too, which we'd open on Christmas morning before my brothers went to Nan and Granddad's house for their dinner, Dad went to the pub and I stayed at home with Mum. It was the same every year, and it was always horrible. Mum didn't ever eat very much, so I don't know if she ate the meal she always cooked on Christmas Day, which I'd eat on my own in the living room, and Dad would have later in the evening when he got back from the pub.

Mum and Dad would both be very drunk by that time, and as soon as Dad got home they'd start to argue and shout at each other. Then that would escalate into a fight, which always resulted in the Christmas tree getting knocked over. There were very few consistencies in my life when I was child; what happened on Christmas Day was one of them.

A few years ago, when I asked my brother Ben what he'd thought at the time about him and Jake – and later Michael – being invited to Nan's house every Christmas while I stayed at home, he said he'd never really thought about it at all. I suppose he was so used to me being an outsider in the family that it just seemed normal. Based on what I found out later about Mum's childhood, one explanation might have been that Nan was trying to protect me, although I'm pretty sure that wasn't the reason, because she didn't like me and because she only ever did anything that benefited her.

Chapter 3

I didn't watch much television as a child. I was usually banished to my room when the rest of the family were watching the videos my parents regularly rented. And although I hated sitting upstairs in solitary confinement, I don't think I resented it: it was just another part of the 'normal' I'd learned to accept. There were a few exceptions to that particular norm, however, such as the time when I was five and Mum let me watch *The Little Mermaid*, which I *loved*, despite the fact that every time she walked past me as I was sitting, transfixed, on the living-room floor, she pulled my hair or pinched me, twisting my skin tightly between her thumb and bony finger, then laughing when I cried out in pain.

I was in the reception class at school at that time and not long after I'd watched *The Little Mermaid*, I found a small, empty perfume bottle in the bathroom, which I slipped into my school bag because it reminded me of her.

At break time that day, I filled the bottle with water and offered my friends a sip of the magic potion that would turn us into mermaids and enable us to live under the sea and have adventures. Before long, a queue of excited children had formed at the water fountain, because although everyone could see that I was just filling an empty bottle with water, it tasted sweet, like fruit and flowers, when they held it to their lips and took a sip.

'It's true,' I heard them telling each other. 'It really is a magic potion.' And eventually I got swept up by their enthusiasm and began to believe it myself, perhaps partly because I so desperately wanted there to be a reality somewhere that was different from the one I was living in. So I was almost as disappointed as they were when playtime came to an end and we all trooped back into the classroom, still children rather than the mermaids and mermen we had expected to be. For me though, it was worth the disappointment to have shared all the excitement and been part of something, even if it had only lasted for one break time.

I learned to read quite quickly after I started school, and by the time I was six I had developed a passion for books that remains with me to this day. For some reason, although I had very few toys, Mum didn't seem to mind me having the books Nan and Granddad gave me, most of which had belonged to her when she was a little girl. So, finally, as my reading skills improved, I had something to do during the hours I spent alone in my bedroom. I still ate supper in my room almost every night, except when Mum didn't bring me any because she was angry or forgot and I went to bed hungry. But even a rumbling tummy can be ignored for a while when you're able to step out of the real world into a Grimm's fairy tale, one of Rudyard Kipling's *Just So Stories*, or any of Roald Dahl's wonderful books.

It was also when I was six that Mum finally gave me permission to use the toilet in the bathroom. I wasn't allowed to wipe my own bottom though; I had to shout for her when I'd finished, then stay on the loo for however long it was before she came. Sometimes I'd be sitting there for ages, until my legs were tingling and numb. When she did finally appear, she'd be even more irritable and impatient than she usually was with me and would make me bend over and touch the floor while she scrubbed my bottom with the rough surface of a sponge she kept in a bucket beside the toilet exclusively for my use.

My brothers thought it was really funny, and Mum used to encourage them, and Dad, to laugh at me, while at the same time making a huge deal of the fact that the bucket and sponge were dirty and disgusting and no one else must ever touch them, which made me feel even more embarrassed and ashamed about having to go to the loo at all.

Sometimes, Jake and Ben would come into the bathroom while I was waiting for Mum, but even though Jake was always very aggressive and I was scared of him, not even his demands to 'Get off the loo, slag. I need to use it' or the threat he made one day that 'I'm going to rape you if you don't get off *now*' would persuade me to risk the beating I knew I would get from Mum if I wasn't sitting there when she eventually came in.

Mum's humiliating bottom-wiping 'game' continued until I was nine years old, by which time I had lost any sense of dignity or self-respect I might otherwise have had and had simply accepted as 'fact' that I was somehow less human and certainly less important than any of the other members of my family. She used to play a lot of humiliating games like that with me. What made them even worse was that everyone believed her when she told them I was incapable of doing even the simplest thing myself because there was something wrong with me mentally. I believed it too eventually, despite the fact that I knew I was perfectly capable of doing everything she claimed I couldn't do.

Not all the videos Mum rented or that we watched on TV were films for children, like *The Little Mermaid*, or old black-and-white films about men being chased and hiding down the sides of buildings. And one day when I was six, Jake and Ben – who always got a great deal of pleasure from scaring me – forced me to watch the video of a TV mini-series called *It* about a sadistic clown who terrorises and kills children. I didn't want to watch it, but just before it started, Jake pushed me down on to the carpet close to the TV, then sat behind me throughout the entire programme with his hands pressing down on my shoulders so I couldn't get up.

It was a terrifying film that was totally unsuitable for children of any age, let alone an anxious little girl who was already frightened of going to bed at night and who looked, in her mind at least, a lot like one of the children who became the clown's victim. I kept closing my eyes and trying to turn my head so that I wouldn't see whatever horrible thing was going to happen next. But every time I looked away from the television, Jake grabbed my hair, pulled my head sharply back and upwards, then punched and slapped me repeatedly in the face until I opened my eyes – and saw what the clown was doing.

The more I whimpered and cried, the more Jake twisted my hair and laughed, refusing to let go even when I started to scream. Mum was in the kitchen and must have heard what was going on, but it was only when the noise I was making began to annoy her that she stormed into the living room, lifted me up off the floor by one arm, dragged me into the kitchen and shouted in my face, 'There's something wrong with you. It's only a man in a mask for fuck's sake.' At just six years old, it was a concept I couldn't grasp, and even if I had been able to, I don't think it would have done anything to lessen the fear that had been implanted in my mind. So I was still crying as I sat in the kitchen with headphones on, listening to music at maximum volume and trying to block out the music from the film, which seemed to have got inside my head.

Although it was Jake who forced me to watch *It* that day, Ben was there too, not saying anything or trying to stop him, perhaps because he was also a bit scared of his older brother. Then, a few days later, Mum and Ben decided to play a 'joke' on me by telling me they'd just seen the clown in the front garden and that he was coming to kill me. I was terrified and could feel my heart thumping even before they pushed me into the hallway and closed the living-room door. While I was sobbing and begging them to let me in, they just laughed and held the door shut, clearly delighted by how successful their prank had been and totally unmoved by my rapid descent into hysterical distress.

A couple of days after that, I went up to my room when I got home from school to find that Mum had bought a new duvet cover for my bed with a picture of a clown on it, who had buttons on his costume that were almost identical to the ones the clown in the film had had. She didn't tell me about it, and I screamed when I opened the door and saw it on my bed. And when I pleaded with her not to make me use it, she just laughed spitefully and told me to 'get used to it'.

It wasn't just Mum who bullied and tormented me when I was a young child. I don't really remember Dad doing it; he laughed at me when she did, and didn't stand up for me as often as he should have done, but mostly he just kept out of things. For example, there was one day when we were sitting in the living room watching TV when Mum suddenly threw herself out of her chair, grabbed me by my hair and started banging my head on the floor. She would often attack me without any provocation or warning, and the reason that particular occasion sticks in my mind is because, as she pinned me to the carpet, with her knee pressing down so heavily on my back that I was struggling to breathe, I saw my dad and two older brothers lean forward and sideways so that they could look around us at the TV.

When Mum eventually stopped hitting me and bashing my head on the floor, she shouted, 'Get upstairs to your room.' And after I'd scrambled to my feet, bruised and crying, I stopped for a moment at the door and turned to look at my dad and brothers, but they didn't even glance in my direction.

'I said get out. Now!' Mum shouted, taking a step towards me and raising her hand as if she was going to hit me again. So I fled upstairs, where I stood at the window in my bedroom, looking out on to the dark street with my palm pressed against the glass, praying silently, 'Can't anyone see me? Someone notice me, please. Someone save me.' Then I crawled into bed, stifling a scream of pain when my head touched the pillow, and sobbed myself to sleep.

I wouldn't have expected my brothers to intervene in a situation like that. But the fact that Dad didn't even seem to notice – and certainly didn't care – that Mum was hurting me felt like further proof that I didn't matter. That was why I was grateful whenever he did mediate on my behalf, because although I could count on the fingers of one hand the number of times he did it, at least I got a clue that although I didn't matter, I didn't always deserve Mum's treatment of me.

The only time Mum ever concealed her dislike of me was when she came to meet me out of school. I was always torn between not wanting to leave the classroom, where I felt safe, and knowing she'd be angry when we got home if I kept her waiting. The fear of her anger always won, and when I walked out into the playground I'd often find her chatting with the other mums and handing out little chocolate bars to some of my friends. She'd give me a chocolate bar too, but I knew it was just for show and that as soon as we got home she'd become 'normal' again.

I'd probably been going to school for a couple of years when a little girl called Rachel must have followed us home one day. I was in the living room when she knocked on the front door, and I heard her ask Mum, 'Is Zoe in? Can she come out?'

'Wait there a minute,' Mum told her, in a voice that was so completely different from her friendly 'playground voice' that although I didn't know *why* I was in trouble, I knew I was. So my heart was already racing when Mum came into the living room and started slapping me with her open hand so viciously I could hardly breathe for sobbing. She was breathless, too, by the time she stopped beating me and said, 'Now go and tell your friend you can't go out.'

Despite my mum's extreme reaction that day, I *was* sometimes allowed to go and play at friends' houses, some of which weren't very different from ours, while others were like something out of another world. Nan and Granddad lived in a council house that was always quite tidy and clean, especially compared with ours, where everything was covered in a thick layer of dust, every room stank of stale cigarette smoke, the carpets were worn and stained, the walls were bare and in need of painting, and all the furniture was mismatched, as if it had been chosen at random by someone with no interest at all in their surroundings, which I suppose was actually true.

It was a contrast that was even more apparent in the gardens, because while Nan and Granddad's was immaculate, ours was even worse than the inside of the house. The only bit of our garden that my brothers and I ever played in was the patch of overgrown grass just outside the back door. Beyond that, there were two rickety sheds Dad had built out of old doors and other discarded debris he'd found in skips, and behind the sheds were a couple of broken fridges, some scrap metal and various other rubbish that had been dumped there over the years to rust and decay.

Despite the fact that the only two houses I'd ever spent any time in before I started school were so totally different, I don't think I was consciously aware that one was clean and the other was dirty, or that one was 'good' and the other 'bad' in some respect – until my friend Carly invited me for tea at her house one day. In Carly's house everything was clean and smelled nice, and we ate our tea sitting at a dining table with her parents, who talked to us and to each other and didn't say anything critical or unpleasant. I had tea at their house several times after that first occasion, and although I don't remember consciously comparing my life to Carly's, I think I must have stored away in my mind the idea that there could be a different, better kind of 'normal' than the one I was used to.

The only thing I didn't like about going to Carly's house was having to eat in front of other people, which I'm still paranoid about today. I always took a packed lunch to school, which I thought was an indication that Mum did love me after all, otherwise why would she bother to make me a sandwich to go with the crisps and cake or chocolate bar in their colour-coordinated packaging. Looking back on it now, I realise it wasn't for my benefit at all: she just wanted my teachers to think she was a good mum. But at least I could eat it all with my hands, which saved me from the embarrassment of having to use a knife and fork. Because although Mum always gave me cutlery when she brought my tea up to my bedroom, no one had ever told me how to use it. So whenever I ate with Carly and her parents, I was always anxious about doing it wrong and used to watch and try to copy what they did, so that I didn't look stupid.

I can remember one day when I was eating at Carly's house and the food kept building up on my knife, making it increasingly difficult for me to cut anything with it. I didn't know how to get it off and I was starting to panic when her dad must have noticed my embarrassment and said, laughing, 'Just lick it off, Zoe. That's what *we* do.' It probably seemed like a small thing to him, saying something to make me feel better, but it meant a lot to me at the time.

I've always had very low self-confidence, which my oldest brother Jake, particularly, played a role in crushing when I was a little girl. Jake and Ben were in their teens by the time I started school and their lives were completely separate from mine. Even before then, I never played with Jake. In fact, I didn't really see much of him at all – which was a good thing as far as I was concerned – because by the time he got back from school every day, I'd already be upstairs in my room, where I'd eat my supper; then he'd often go out again with his mates and not come home until after I was in bed. When I did see him, he usually ignored me, which, again, was a good thing from my point of view because he only ever said nasty things to me or paid me any attention because he was angry.

I know Ben and Michael were scared of him and I think my parents were wary of him too, because he had a very bad temper. In fact, he made several holes in the walls and door of the room he shared with Ben and Michael by smashing his fist into them when he was in a rage.

Ben wasn't violent like Jake was, but I didn't have much contact with him either – even seven years is quite a significant age difference when you're a child. I do have a couple of nice memories of him though, like the time he came to meet me from school one day and gave me a ride home on his push bike, which made me think he cared about me. Sometimes, when Jake was out, Ben used to let me sit on his bed and watch him drawing, and he'd talk to me when he took me into town to get my hair cut, or ask me questions about what I'd been doing at school.

He made a paper bird for me once too. It had wings like fans and he stuck it to the ceiling of my bedroom with a bit of cotton he took out of Mum's drawer, which she'd have been angry about if she'd found out. I thought it was brilliant. But Mum made him take it down when she saw it, because the Sellotape would damage the paint, she said, although that clearly wasn't the real reason, because, like the rest of the house, my room was in need of decorating and another bit of peeling paint wouldn't have made any difference.

I didn't ever actually play with Ben though, like I did with Michael as he got a bit older. Eventually though, Mum did what she was always did if anything ever looked as though it might turn out well for me – she intervened to change the course of events by trying her best to destroy my relationship with Michael, and by the time he was seven years old he sometimes called me names too, just like Mum and my older brothers had always done. And although I tried to tell myself it wasn't his fault, it hurt me far more than Jake's taunting and sneering ever did.

I know that lots of children are bullied by their siblings. Perhaps when kept within reasonable limits it becomes part of the process of learning what's acceptable behaviour and what isn't and how to deal with being teased. Maybe some parents don't allow it at all, and some probably don't even notice it's happening, whereas others, like mine – or like my mum, at least – actively encourage it.

It went way beyond 'just a bit of sibling bullying' with Jake though. For example, there was one day, a few months after I'd been forced to watch that first horrific film about the clown, when Ben, Jake and I were in the garden and Jake suddenly took a step towards me, sliced the air between us with the long-handled knife he'd been using to cut the tall, weed-infested grass and said, 'I could chop off your head with this and nobody would care.' There was no humour in his expression when he said it and his eyes were hard as he turned to Ben and added, 'I could tell Dad it was an accident. He'd believe me if you backed me up.'

Ben looked really scared when he said, 'Okay.' And I was scared too, because I really did think they were going to do it and I knew what Jake had said was true – Dad *would* believe them and nobody *would* care.

Chapter 4

I never relaxed or enjoyed anything when I was at home. Everything I did was wrong and the only time anyone ever really spoke to me was to tell me off. So it had been a completely new and unimagined experience going to school and discovering that there was a world where I wasn't an unwanted, unloved outcast, and where sometimes an adult actually praised me for getting something right.

I don't know if it was the realisation that I wasn't always wrong, or as stupid as my mum always told me I was, that made me love learning. 'Zoe soaks up knowledge like a sponge,' my teacher wrote in one of my early school reports, which made me feel proud of myself for the first time. So then I worked even harder, behaved even better and did everything else I could think of to please my teachers so that they'd say the magic words, 'Good girl, Zoe.'

Not everything about school was positive, however. Some of the teachers I had during those first few years helped me a lot, but there was one who was horrible. Miss Heston was my form teacher when I was seven and she had some very odd ideas about how to teach and interact with young children. One incident I remember particularly occurred when I pinched the arm of one of my classmates because he said he had sunburn. I don't know why I did it, but it obviously hurt him quite a lot and when he told the teacher what I'd done, she made everyone in the class sit down, then said, 'Zoe Patterson, come and stand by my desk.'

I hated being the centre of any kind of attention, but particularly if I was in trouble, and as I stood at the front of the classroom, twisting my fingers nervously and staring at my feet, she told me, 'I'm going to show you what that feels like.' And before I realised what she was going to do, she grabbed my arm and started giving me a Chinese burn.

Presumably her intention was to inflict on me a pain similar to the one I'd inflicted on the boy with sunburn when I'd pinched him. In which case, she'd have been pleased to know that the Chinese burn really hurt. But I'd had years of practice holding back tears and I was determined not to humiliate myself in front of all the other kids in my class, and not to give my teacher the satisfaction of seeing me cry. Mum often used to try to reduce me to tears when she was hurting me, and I always knew that she'd hurt me even more if I cried, and would eventually lose interest and give up if I didn't. For my teacher, however, my stoicism seemed to have the opposite effect, and after watching me closely for a few seconds as she twisted the skin on my scrawny arm, she suddenly swung me across her knee and started slapping the backs of my legs.

I heard some of the children gasp when she did it, and someone gave a single high-pitched bark of laughter. Then the room fell completely silent except for the sound of the teacher's open hand smacking my bare legs, until eventually she snapped at me, 'Go and sit down,' and I struggled to my feet. The skin on my wrist and the backs of my legs was burning as I walked unsteadily back to my seat, but there was a small glow of satisfaction inside me too, because I'd managed not to shed a single one of the tears that had been building up behind my eyes from the moment she'd called me out to the front of the classroom.

It never crossed my mind to tell my parents when something like that happened at school. After all, I *had* hurt the little boy, so it really was my fault and I'd got what I deserved, just like I so often did at home, although with at least some underlying justification on this occasion. To me, what happened that day at school was simply a variation of 'normal' and not worth mentioning to anyone. And I knew my parents wouldn't have *done* anything about it if I had told them, except Mum might have beaten me again for getting into trouble with my teacher.

I already knew Miss Heston didn't like me. She made it clear in lots of ways, such as on the day she put a box of hats on the floor in the middle of the classroom and told us all to pick the one that matched the job we'd like to do when we left school. It's difficult to imagine yourself as an adult when you're seven, and perhaps even more difficult to visualise having a job. But in amongst all the hats there was a jockey's cap, and as I liked the idea of being able to ride a horse, I picked it up and was just about to put it on my head when I noticed a black hat with a chequered band and a silver badge, like a police officer would wear. 'Maybe that would be even better than being a jockey,' I thought, reaching for the black hat with one hand while replacing the jockey's cap with the other, just as Miss Heston slapped my arm and said, 'No, Zoe Patterson. Leave it. You've made your choice.'

So I kept the jockey's cap and went to stand by the wall where we'd been told to line up to have a photograph taken. Then, just as I was putting it on my head, my hair-band slipped down in front of my eyes and when I raised my hand to tug it back into place, Miss Heston snapped at me again saying, 'Don't pull it up. It can stay like that,' and took the photo. I still have that photograph and whenever I look at it, it reminds me of Miss Heston and makes me wonder why she was like that. Because it wasn't just me she was mean to; there were other kids who regularly got into trouble too, like the boy she pushed into a sort of bookcase one day because he'd been swearing, then slammed the door on him repeatedly, while we all watched with a mixture of sympathy and guilt – or at least I know I did, because I was glad it was him and not me being punished on that occasion.

There *was* one positive aspect to having Miss Heston as our teacher, however, because my older brothers had had her too, and Ben and I used to swap stories about the things she did. For example, when Ben was in her class she put strands of her hair in the goldfish tank to prove that it's a bad thing to do because it gets caught in the fishes' gills and suffocates them; and sometimes she'd put a sweet in her mouth, then take it out and insist on some child who'd had been naughty eating it. Ben would laugh at the expression on my face when he told me things like that, and I'd laugh too, because I liked the feeling of having even that brief point of contact, which was something we hadn't ever really had before. It was just a shame that the year I spent in Miss Heston's class made it even more difficult for me to distinguish between normal and abnormal behaviour, and that I ended the year with even lower self-esteem than I'd had when I started it.

Fortunately, most of my other teachers were more balanced and encouraging, and when I was nine I had a really nice one, who encouraged me and gave me work for science that the older children were doing and that I found really interesting. It was when I was in his class that I was sitting in the garden at home one day working on some homework he'd set me when Mum came out and asked what I was doing.

'I have to write down what time I see the moon,' I told her. 'My teacher said you can see it in the daytime as well as when it's dark.'

'You're fucking stupid,' Mum told me scornfully. 'The moon doesn't come out in the day. Everyone knows that. Except you and your stupid teacher apparently.' Then she stomped back into the house, muttering her contempt.

But the moon did come out while it was still light. I saw it. And I was glad that Mum had been wrong and my teacher was right. It felt like a small triumph, and I think it might also have sown a seed of doubt in my mind about some of Mum's other 'facts' and made me think that if she was wrong about the moon, maybe there were other things she was wrong about too.

During that year when I was nine, Jake was 18 and had left school, Ben was 16 and doing his GCSEs, and Michael must have been five. The three of them still slept in the same room, and one night Jake came home drunk and put the stereo on loudly so that it woke everyone up. Ben was a bit shorter than Jake and quite skinny, and the reason I remember it particularly is because it was the first time I'd ever seen him stand up to his older brother. I suppose it was because he was in the middle of taking his exams, which he worked hard for because he wanted to do well and go to university. And after he'd put his fist through the speaker in their bedroom, he and Jake went outside – at my parents' insistence – and fought it out.

It must have been around that same time that I was doing my homework one evening when Ben told me I could borrow his pen. 'It's on the desk in our room,' he said. 'Just go up and get it.'

I'd just picked it up and was turning away from the desk when Jake came in and shouted at me, 'What the fuck are *you* doing?' He'd already taken a few steps into the bedroom before he realised I was there, and there was a clear but narrow passage between me and the open door. So, before he could stop me, I darted past him, across the landing and into my bedroom, where I just managed to shut the door before he started thumping on it with his fists.

Although Jake isn't very tall, he was always quite chunky, and certainly much bigger and heavier at 18 than I was at nine. *And* he was angry. So although I threw all my weight against the door and tried desperately to hold it shut, it wasn't very difficult for him to force it open, and send me flying across the room. I was still trying to scramble to my feet when he picked me up by my hair and punched me in the face, splitting my lip and filling my mouth with blood.

Ben came upstairs a few minutes later and when he saw me standing in the bathroom with a blood-stained wad of toilet paper pressed against my mouth, he told me, 'It'll be all right. Just go back to your room and close the door.' And that was the only thing that was said by anyone about what Jake had done to me.

The following year, when I was ten, Dad was made redundant, and it wasn't long before my life at home had become even more miserable and difficult to cope with.

I can't remember when Dad first started saying peculiar things to me. I always hated it, even when I didn't know what he meant when he said things like, 'You shouldn't wear any clothes when you're in bed,' or pointed to my private parts and asked, 'Do you know what that is?' What I hated even more, however, were the creepy gestures he made and the way he flicked his tongue in and out of his mouth while sticking his chin out and looking at me sideways.

Mum thought his comments and gestures were funny – when they were directed at me – and she'd warned me almost every night for as long as I could remember, 'Be careful of wandering hands in your bed tonight. You don't want to wake up and feel them touching you.' She'd smile her nasty smile when she said it, then switch immediately back to being angry as she added, 'Just you remember though: you stay in your bed until *I* say you can get out.'

She always laughed when she knew she'd frightened me, and I was always frightened when I was in bed, even before I knew that the wandering hands she was warning me about were my dad's.

Dad had been making lewd gestures and saying inappropriate things to me for years. I didn't understand their sexual connotations when I was younger, I just found them creepy and disturbing. But it got worse after he had to give up work and was at home – or at the pub – all the time, and he started doing things like sitting in the living room with his flies undone and asking me to sit on his knee, which I always refused to do.

Ironically, after spending so many hours of my childhood alone in my bedroom wishing I could be part of the family, I longed to go up to my room when he was being like that, but Mum wouldn't let me. Sometimes, there'd be something on TV to do with sex that I didn't want to see, and while I tried to block the screen so that my little brother couldn't see it either, Dad would keep asking me if I knew what the people were doing. Then he'd blow kisses at me and gesture with his fingers and tongue in a way that made me feel dirty and vulnerable.

Mum started sleeping on the sofa every night after Dad was made redundant, so he slept alone in their bedroom, which was next to mine, and I could hear him masturbating at night, which really frightened me, because although I didn't know what he was doing, I thought he was going to do something to hurt me.

He drank more than ever after he was made redundant, and I can remember being really scared every time I had a bath in case he came home from the pub while I was in it and insisted on coming into the bathroom to use the toilet. I would have my back to the toilet when I was in the bathtub, and however long he took to have his pee or however loudly he grunted and groaned, I didn't ever turn around.

The one time Mum did try to get him out, she came in when he was using the toilet and started shouting at him, and it ended up with them screaming at each other, then having what sounded like a physical fight at the top of the stairs. Even then I didn't turn around, and as I wouldn't have dreamed of getting out of the bath without Mum's permission, I just had to sit there as the water got colder and colder, waiting for them to stop yelling and hitting each other.

What made everything even worse was that while Dad's behaviour towards me was becoming weirder and more suggestive, Mum continued to warn me to 'Watch out for hands in your bed'. Then Dad started hitting me too, which he'd never really done before, and although he didn't ever do it as regularly as Mum had always done, he did sometimes bruise and hurt me, like the time he used a plastic pool cue from my brother's mini pool table to beat the back of my thighs and calves, injuring me so severely I couldn't walk properly for a week. I can't remember why he did it; probably just because he was drunk.

Later that same year when Dad was made redundant, Granddad died of a sudden heart attack and Mum started sending me to Nan's every Saturday. I hated having to spend the day with my nan, not least because she never spoke to me and wouldn't let me speak either. She used to chatter away to my brothers all the time, and even took them on holidays with her, so I thought it must be my fault that she didn't like me.

There was one good thing about those Saturdays, however, which was that Nan would take me to the library. Even then she wasn't actually nice to me, and if I started to say something to her while we were on the bus, she would cut across me and snap, 'No! You are *not* to talk.' She always said it loud enough for people to hear, which was really embarrassing and made me feel stupid, so then I'd spend the rest of the journey trying to avoid making eye contact with anyone. It was only later that I realised the real reason for those trips to the library was so that I would have something to occupy me when she made me sit in silence for the rest of day.

I didn't see my grandparents very often before Granddad died, so I don't think his death had a particularly significant impact on me. It did seem to affect Mum though, or maybe it was Dad not working and being at home more often that caused her to start beating me even more viciously than she'd done before.

There was one day when she burst into the bathroom while I was on the toilet and hit me so ferociously with the heel of her shoe that she knocked me off the seat and on to the floor. She didn't say why she was so angry with me, and after she'd stormed out of the bathroom again, I just lay there for a few minutes, wondering what I'd done wrong.

It wasn't unusual for her not to give a reason for punishing me. In fact, I rarely knew why either of my parents was furious with me, or understood why they blamed me for everything and seemed to dislike me so much – Dad too by that time. And because I usually didn't know what I'd done wrong, I didn't know how to do it right.

I was still lying on the bathroom floor trying to work it all out when I noticed a little plastic shaver on the side of the bath. I don't remember even thinking about what I was doing as I grasped the edge of the bathtub with both hands, pulled myself up into a sitting position, reached across to pick up the razor, and made a couple of quick cuts on my knee. I know I was angry too by that time, and that I'd suddenly felt overwhelmed by an almost physical sense of despair. So maybe, subconsciously, I thought that releasing blood from my own body might release some of the pressure that felt as though it had built up inside me to an almost unbearable level.

Whatever the reason, it did feel like a release, even though the cuts I made on my knee that first time were only superficial and stopped bleeding quite quickly. I must have been a bit frightened by what I'd done though, because when I went to school the next day, I showed the cuts to a friend and told her about Mum hitting me with her shoe. I didn't normally talk to anyone about anything that happened at home, but by the time I was ten years old I was finding it increasingly difficult to cope. So I think that by telling my friend Fiona and asking her to tell our teacher, I was hoping someone would step in to help me.

'She didn't believe me,' Fiona said when I saw her the next morning. 'She said I mustn't talk about things like that.'

We had moved up into the next class by that time, and no longer had the really nice teacher who'd encouraged my interest in science. Our new teacher was okay though, so I was a bit surprised when she didn't say anything to me about what my friend had told her, and it wasn't until some time later that it crossed my mind to wonder if Fiona actually did speak to her.

I'd seen several frightening films since Jake forced me to watch the one about the clown – *A Nightmare on Elm Street*, for example, and *Child's Play*, which is about a serial killer whose soul gets into a really scary doll called Chucky. I hated them all and never watched any of them willingly, but sometimes Jake insisted and sometimes there'd be one on TV when my mum decided I had to be downstairs. Again, I don't think I realised that making a young child sit through films like that wasn't normal, until I was in the corridor at school one day telling a friend about something I'd seen and a teacher who was standing nearby suddenly spun round and said, 'Zoe Patterson, that's horrible! Don't ever let me hear you talking about that sort of thing again.'

Looking back on it now, she probably should have asked me how I knew about stuff like that. If she had, I might have told her, then perhaps it would have all come out. But she didn't say anything else, and I didn't either.

It was after that incident I started to off-load some of the horrific scenes that were lodged in my mind by writing horror stories, which I took in to school and showed my teacher. It was all really scary stuff, mostly with plots based on films I'd seen, although sometimes with a twist. For example, there was one about Chucky the doll coming into our school and killing all the teachers, which I think was the one that finally prompted *my* teacher to say, 'Enough! If you can't write about something nice, don't write anything at all.'

I know it must have seemed odd to anyone else – the sort of thing a little girl in a horror film might do perhaps – but I enjoyed writing those stories; it was an escape for me, like reading. And, somehow, the fact that I was able to make up scary stories made the films seem a bit less frightening, although even today I still sometimes have nightmares about the clown in *It*. So I was really upset by what my teacher said and I stopped writing altogether after that.

I think I had already started losing confidence at school and becoming more withdrawn by that time. Things at home were getting worse too, because Dad's behaviour was becoming increasingly odd and he had started insisting he wasn't well and phoning for an ambulance. I don't know what he said to make the ambulance come – I think he complained about something to do with his heart. But they always did come, and then always left again after checking him out, saying there wasn't anything they could do for him.

It got so bad in the end that Dad's brother and his wife came to our house one day to try to talk to him about what was happening, but he wouldn't let them do anything to help him. I don't know if it was Mum who got in touch with them. If it was, it would only have been because he was driving her crazy. She certainly never showed him any sympathy or tried to talk to him about what was wrong. She was just angry with him all the time and would shout things at him like, 'What the fuck's up with you, you stupid bastard?'

Mum and Dad were arguing almost constantly by that time, which was another reason why I didn't mind when Mum started to encourage me to stay in my room again. 'It's best this way,' she would say when she brought my supper up to me, 'so that you can avoid your dad.' Which seemed to make sense.

In any case, all I really wanted to do was sleep. My brothers just laughed at me and said I was 'mental', while Mum seemed to enjoy watching me slide deeper and deeper into depression. I don't know whether anyone realised there was actually something wrong with me. Perhaps not, because Mum didn't ever speak to me except to feed the fear I had of my dad. In fact, she didn't even say anything when I started to leave the food she brought up to my room, which at any other time would have made her really angry.

I don't think I realised I was depressed either, although I was certainly aware that I was struggling to cope. Then, one day, I came home from school and Mum told me, 'Your dad's not well. He's had a breakdown.' She didn't explain what that meant, although I think I guessed it might be something to do with 'things not being right in his head', which is what she always used to say about him, particularly after he was made redundant.

It turned out that he'd been admitted to hospital while I was at school that day, and even after Mum had taken my little brother Michael and me to see him there a few times, I still didn't understand what was going on. I just remember bursting into tears at school on a couple of occasions, then talking to a teacher about it. What I didn't ever tell anyone, however, is that one of the things I found really upsetting was waving goodbye to Dad after we'd visited him in the hospital, because it reminded me of waving to him as he left the house to go to work when I was a small child. It still makes me cry when I think about it today, and about how the dad I used to love turned into someone so totally different.

What was also very upsetting about those visits to the hospital was the fact that he didn't acknowledge us or even seem to know we were there. So, after a while, Mum stopped taking us to see him. I know it sounds horrible to say that it was a relief not having him at home for those three months, but it was, because at least I didn't have to worry about 'wandering hands' in my bed or listen to my parents shouting and fighting with each other.

Dad didn't ever work again after that. He was quite a bit older than Mum and I think he was only a few years off retirement age when he had what she refers to as 'his breakdown'. After he came out of hospital, he just sat around the house all day drinking, arguing with Mum, and saying things to me that I began to understand better as I got older and that made me afraid that one day he might stop just talking about it and sexually abuse me.

Chapter 5

Despite struggling to cope with everything that was going on at home, I did make some friends when I moved up to the high school, where I did quite well academically too. Then Dad's sister died and he had to clear out her house, which caused more trouble at home and didn't do anything to help his mental state, especially when he ended up having to bring a lot of her stuff back to our house and Mum gave him a really hard time about it.

Dad had been close to his sister. They'd kept in touch over the years, even though we didn't see them very often, and after he came out of hospital and things got worse between him and Mum, he started going to stay with her at weekends and going out for meals with the cousins I've never really known. Eating out was something our family had never done and I think it was like another life for him, perhaps the sort of life he'd have been living if he hadn't met and married Mum.

It makes me very sad to think that Dad might have missed the opportunity to be the person he could have been. And it must have been really difficult for him trying to cope with everything after his sister's death without any support or sympathy from Mum, who used to scream at him when he brought stuff home, 'You can't bring all that crap in here. You can't fit two houses into one, you stupid bastard.'

One of the things Dad brought from my aunt's house was a step machine, which Mum suggested I should put behind my bedroom door at night. 'I saw your dad watching you while you were asleep,' she told me. 'If you pull that in front of your door when you go to bed, he won't be able to open it.' So every night before I got into bed, I dragged the heavy step machine into place, then lay there listening for the sound of the door banging against it. I heard Ben asked Mum one day why I did it, to which she replied, 'Oh just ignore her. She does daft things. You know that.' But I still thought she'd allowed me to put the step machine in my room because she was trying to protect me and keep me safe from my dad.

When I was 12, I started having flashbacks. They seemed to be of real events that had occurred when I was younger and were always very disturbing, even though they didn't make any sense. For example, in one of them I was wearing a nappy and sitting on the baby gate that used to block off the doorway between the living room and kitchen when I was a toddler. Mum was there, but it was

Granddad who lifted me up and put me on top of the gate so that I was straddling it with one leg on either side. Then he pushed me down somehow, so that the top of the gate was rubbing against my private parts.

It sounds daft, I know, and I probably would have forgotten all about it by now if it hadn't been for the fact that when I mentioned it to Mum some years later, she told me, almost defensively, 'It was just a game. You loved him doing that. He did it all the time.' So then I knew it was a real memory, although in view of everything else I knew by that time, it did seem like a very odd thing for her to have allowed him to do.

One of the other flashbacks I started having seemed to be related more to a feeling than to what was actually happening. Nan was there and I was sitting on my granddad's knee – I think it was at my grandparents' house – and Granddad had his hand up my skirt. During the brief moment when the image was clear in my mind, I had an overpowering sense of being upset and not wanting him to do whatever it was he was doing. But, again, it didn't make any sense.

Once the flashbacks started, I began to remember other things too, like the bikini and other clothes Nan used to dress me up in when I was four or five years old, and her telling me, 'You mustn't say anything to anyone about these special clothes.' Then Granddad took photographs of me standing with my legs open and doing other poses he told me to do, which weren't the sort of poses I'd have done naturally as a little girl and which made me feel awkward and uncomfortable, although I didn't know why.

I've still got one of the photographs Granddad took when I'd gone with him to visit one of his friends one day. It's a perfectly innocent-looking photograph – I'm sitting on a piano stool with a little lad who was also at the house – and I never understood why it made my skin crawl whenever I looked at it, as though there was something creepy associated with it. So in the end I put it away.

Although those visits to my grandparents' house stopped when I was five or six years old, I must have gone out with them sometimes after that, because I remember being with them and my little brother one day when Michael fell over. Granddad said he'd take him in to the toilet to clean him up, but I insisted on doing it myself, because I had a horrible feeling that if he went with Granddad, something bad might happen to him, although I couldn't have said what.

For me, the flashbacks were the straw that broke the camel's back – the final extra burden that made the weight of everything I was carrying too much to bear. So I did what my parents had always done and started trying to drown my sorrows in drink.

Although I was very scared of Jake, the first alcohol I ever drank was one of his cans of lager, which I stole from my brothers' bedroom. It didn't taste very nice, but the purpose of drinking it wasn't to enjoy it, and it *did* stop the flashbacks for a while. So then I started stealing whisky from the bottles Mum always had in the house. I knew I was taking a huge risk and that she'd be really angry with me if she found out what I was doing. But, in fact, I was wrong, because when she did find out, she just laughed, poured out two glasses and handed one to me.

I was 12 years old, in my second year at high school, and happy to drink a glass of whisky with my mum because I thought it meant I had finally found some common ground between us that might enable me to start building the relationship with her I had always longed to have.

She gave me cola and whisky quite regularly after that, and would often bring a glass up to my room when I was sitting there alone in the evenings. By the time I was 13, she was giving me a 500-ml cola bottle full of equal measures of cola and whisky to take to school every morning, telling me cheerily as she handed it to me, 'Remember, if you get caught, don't tell them you got it from me!' Which I took to be further proof that we were bonding, because it was the first time she had ever given me something I wanted, rather than doing everything in her power to make sure I didn't get it.

Sometimes, after she started giving me whisky, she'd give me money to buy lager too. Then I'd hang around outside a local shop after school, waiting for some likely-looking person to come along who I could ask to go in and buy me a couple of cans, which someone always did.

Then, one day, Mum told me Dad had raped her while I was at school. 'It's your fault,' she said. 'He wouldn't have done it if you'd been here.' So I started skipping school sometimes, and because she was still encouraging me to stay in my room, particularly at weekends and during the school holidays, I would sit up there on my own drinking my bottle of cola and whisky and listening, in case my mother needed me.

Since my first day at nursery, school had been the one place I could escape to, and I'd always done quite well – until I started getting into trouble sometimes for being drunk, which I almost always was by the end of the day. Even then, nobody really did anything. And after a while taking whisky to school stopped being funny, like a teen-age prank or a dare, and became something that isolated me from my friends and made me incapable of doing my work properly. Before long, I was drinking about 250 ml of whisky and cola every school day, plus strong lager in the evenings, or whatever else I could get someone to buy for me when I'd saved up enough money from the couple of pounds Dad sometimes gave me. He didn't know I was spending it on drink because he was in his own world by that time, and having rarely smiled before his breakdown, never did so now.

Eventually, I was having to drink more and more alcohol to find the dead space inside my head where nothing mattered, and I would sometimes steal from Mum's stash of whisky. But again, instead of being angry with me when she found out, she started buying me two bottles a week and occasionally, if she was in a really good mood, she'd let me have one of her cans of strong lager too. We didn't ever sit and drink it together – the desire to bond was mine, not Mum's – but she used to tell me it would help me not to feel so anxious about what I thought my dad might be going to do to me. So although she always laughed when he said lewd things to me, I told myself that she really did care. And when the alcohol stopped suppressing the flashbacks, I started self-harming.

I had only done it once before, tentatively, with the razor I'd found in the bathroom when I was ten. But soon I was cutting myself with anything sharp I could find – a knife from the kitchen, a Stanley knife, a razor, a set of compasses … I always kept the cuts and scars hidden, until one day – I suppose because I knew it was getting it out of hand – I rolled up one of my sleeves and showed my arm to my brother Ben.

'Why?' Ben asked me, his expression of shock turning to revulsion as he took hold of my wrist and gently rotated it.

I didn't know how to explain the feeling I had every time I ran a blade across my skin and watched the blood ooze from between the cut surfaces. 'Because it makes me feel as though I've exhaled after holding my breath for too long,' I could have told him. But I knew he wouldn't understand – I didn't understand it myself. So I just shrugged, then pulled down my sleeve and said, 'I don't know.'

I can't remember if I actually asked Ben not to tell Mum. Maybe not, if showing him the cuts *was* a cry for help and a way of passing on the responsibility for what I was doing to someone else. I don't think he told her because he was trying to get me into trouble though. I think he was panicking and didn't know what else to do. And a couple of minutes later she came stomping up to my room shouting, 'What the fuck are you doing, you stupid bitch? There's something wrong with you. You're evil.'

'Mum, don't! Don't shout at her.' Ben appeared in the doorway behind her, his face still white with shock. But she ignored him, and continued her tirade of furious abuse.

Mum had always encouraged me to believe that the only place in my home where I was safe was in my bedroom, and as I became more anxious and less able to cope, it was the only place I ever really wanted to be. So I stopped going out with any of my friends – which I'd only done occasionally before then – and gradually became completely cut off from everyone.

I can remember thinking that I seemed suddenly to have lost all control of my emotions: if I was sad, I cried; if I was angry, I got into arguments with my teachers and with other kids at school. So it wasn't long before no one wanted to have anything to do with me either, and after having been a relatively safe haven for the last nine years, school became somewhere I didn't want to be, although I did continue to go on some days.

Apart from the one time I showed the cuts to my brother, I always kept my arms covered so that no one could see the ugly red lines that criss-crossed the skin or the scars they left when they healed. I think I had some vague idea that eventually someone would be able to see that I was depressed and desperate, and then I'd get the help I needed. But as the days turned into weeks, then months, and still nothing changed, I decided to show the cuts on my arms to my English teacher.

I didn't want my parents to get into trouble, so all I told her was, 'I'm just not happy at home.' But although she was sympathetic, she said there was nothing she could really do to help me. So then I told my form tutor, 'My mum hits me,' and started going to the office at school sometimes to talk to the welfare officer. And although the welfare officer did apparently contact social services, they told her that whatever the problem was, the school would have to deal with it.

I'd added solvent abuse to the drinking and self-harming by that time, and was regularly getting into trouble at school. So, for me, the most immediate problem that needed to be dealt with was the fact that every time I got caught drinking or sniffing glue on school premises, my parents would be informed, my mum would beat me when I got home, I would run away, then I'd have to go home again because I had nowhere else to go, she would beat me again, I would think about taking my own life ... and the vicious circle would continue.

The welfare officer did tell me that she was trying to get a social worker to come and see me, and when one did eventually come to the school to talk to me, I told her, 'I'm not safe at home. I don't want to live with my parents any more. I've always thought everything was my fault. But now I don't know. I don't think I've done anything to deserve being treated so badly. I keep thinking about killing myself. Not because I *want* to die. I just can't think of any other way to make it all stop.'

After a lifetime of not daring to tell anyone about what was happening to me at home, it felt very scary to be talking about it at all. In any other circumstances, I simply wouldn't have taken the risk, because of what I knew my mum would do to me if she found out. But I truly believed that if I told the social worker, she would take me somewhere I'd be safe and cared for – maybe even loved. So it felt like the end of the road when she said, 'I'll see what I can do,' then everything continued the way it had always been.

I think my teachers were doing their best to help me – some of them, at least – by informing social services about any incidents they became aware of, and in the end I was assigned a social worker called Valerie Hampton, who came to talk to me at home.

A very tall woman in her mid- to late twenties with broad shoulders, big hands and feet, short hair that was dyed a dark henna colour, and a very distinctive nasal voice, my first impression of Valerie Hampton was that she saw herself as the sort of social worker who 'gets' young people. To me though, however friendly she might have been, it doesn't seem very logical to expect a child to be able to talk openly about the reasons they feel unsafe at home *while they're at home*! I still felt very protective of my mum too, so I didn't say much except what I'd said before to my form teacher – that Mum sometimes hit me.

'Huh! *She's* the problem,' Mum told the social worker, glaring at me as she spoke. '*She's* the one who causes all the trouble in *this* family. There's something wrong with her. She lies about everything.'

It's the sort of thing you'd probably expect anyone to say when they've been accused of something like that. But Mum must have been more convincing than I was, because I found out later that Valerie Hampton decided I was attention seeking and making it all up, although she didn't seem to ask herself why. Perhaps what also helped to persuade her was my nan getting involved by phoning social services and telling them I was mentally ill, which I also only discovered later.

Eventually, however, I was assessed by someone from Child and Adolescent Mental Health Services (CAMHS), who said I had reactive depression – I think that's what they called it – but that they couldn't help me until I was in a safe environment. And still nothing was done. So I ended up being off school for about eight weeks, during which time I spent every day and night in my bedroom, sleeping or just staring into space, knowing I couldn't cope anymore, but not being able to think of any way that I might be able to change the situation I was in.

Once, when I'd begun to feel like a caged animal and on the verge of a panic attack, I ran away to a friend's house and asked if I could stay there. Her parents said I could, then phoned Mum to let her know where I was. So then she and Dad came round, and as soon as she walked in the front door she kicked off, telling my friend's parents, 'There's something wrong with Zoe. She needs to be put in an institution. I don't know why you're even bothering with her.' While Dad just kept saying, 'It's all right, Zoe. You can come home. No one's going to hit you.' Which isn't something you'd expect a parent to have to say to their child, although the possibility that by saying it he was rather proving what *I'd* said didn't seem to cross his mind.

In the end, I stayed with my friend and her family for a couple of days before going home for a few days, then running away again to stay with another friend, whose parents would have let me live with them for longer if I hadn't been drinking and had all the other 'issues' my social worker told me it wasn't fair to inflict on them.

I found out later that my friend's mum had told my social worker she was concerned about me because I seemed to be withdrawn and got very anxious whenever they asked me to sit in the living room with them. The fact was, I was so used to being unwanted by my own family that I felt like an intruder in someone else's home and didn't believe they really wanted me to be with them. I feel sad about that now, because her parents were very good to me, and I wasn't able to accept their kindness.

After Valerie Hampton came to our house, social services did an assessment of Mum and Dad too. I'd told Mum about the flashbacks I'd been having of some of the things Granddad used to do to me, and she told the social worker, perhaps because she wanted to cover herself in case any of it ever came out. I can't think of any other reason why Valerie Hampton asked me one day if I knew that baby girls get pleasure from rubbing their genitals against the straps of their prams. I hadn't ever said anything to *her* that might have prompted her to ask me such an embarrassing question. So maybe Mum had given her a doctored version of what I'd said about Granddad.

I don't know whether Mum was very clever or whether the social worker was just naive – perhaps a bit of both, because social services were certainly fooled into believing that everything that happened at home was my fault. Which isn't surprising, I suppose, when you consider the fact that Mum had made me believe it too, for 13 years.

'I've given her a good hiding in the past,' she told the social worker, presumably realising it was better to admit some of the things I'd talked about rather than deny them all. 'It's not us though,' she said. 'There's something wrong with her. She needs medical help. She spends most of her time barricaded in her bedroom.' Which seemed particularly unfair, when barricading myself in my bedroom had been *her* suggestion, after she'd done everything else she could think of to make me fear and suspect my dad.

I don't think the social worker wanted to have to deal with any of it. To her, it was probably just a case of an attention-seeking teenage girl not wanting to live by the rules imposed by parents who sometimes became so frustrated with their daughter's difficult behaviour they lashed out at her. Eventually though, she did get the National Society for the Prevention of Cruelty to Children involved and I had been put on a waiting list for counselling when she came to the house one day with someone from the charity.

My social worker, the woman from the NSPCC, Dad, Mum and I all sat in the living room, with Dad saying nothing while the two women asked questions, which were answered with half-truths by me and with blatant lies by Mum. Then the two women clicked their Biros, closed their notepads and shuffled their papers into neat piles, and suddenly the only thing that mattered was that they didn't walk out of the house and leave me there.

'I've got bruises from where Mum beat me,' I said, rolling up one leg of my trousers quickly when everyone turned to look at me.

'Is this true, Mrs Patterson?' The woman from the NSPCC looked shocked when she saw the black, purple and yellow marks that almost completely covered my calf and shin. 'Did you hit your daughter and cause that bruising?'

I was holding my breath, expecting Mum to explain, in the fake-reasonable voice she'd adopted while answering all their other questions, that I was somehow responsible for my own injuries. But the strain of pretending she was a rational human being had obviously proved too much and she started screaming, 'Don't you fucking look at me like that, you stupid bitch. She's lying. I told you: she's fucking mental.' And, finally, they saw her as she really was.

'I think it would be a good idea for Zoe to live somewhere else for a while,' the social worker said when Mum eventually calmed down enough to be able to hear her. 'Just for a few weeks, while we do an assessment. It'll be on a voluntary basis. So you'll still have a say in any decisions that need to be made on her behalf.'

I don't know if she said it because she really believed my parents cared about what happened to me. But Mum refused to give her permission for me to be taken into care – just to be awkward rather than because she didn't want me to go, or perhaps because she was afraid of what else I might tell social services once she no longer had any direct control over me – and when she stormed out of the living room, Dad signed the forms.

'I'll come back later this afternoon,' the social worker said as the two women tidied their papers and closed their notepads again, 'after I've sorted out somewhere for you to go, Zoe. Just pack what you'll need for the next few days.'

I was elated at the thought of getting away from my home and family, even if it wasn't going to be forever. But

I was also very anxious about being left there with Mum after what I'd just said and done. For some reason, however, she didn't follow me when I went up to my bedroom to grab what I thought I might need and shove it into my school bag. In fact, she stayed in the kitchen and didn't speak to me at all until the social worker came back a couple of hours later, when she shouted at me, 'You better not have taken my fucking hairbrush.' And that was the last thing she said to me before I was taken into care.

I discovered some years later that the social worker had made a note in my file to the effect that my mother was 'very verbally abusive' towards me. Mum's parting words did have some relevance, however – in her mind at least – because having never had a hairbrush of my own, I would sometimes use hers. What *is* interesting, in retrospect, is the fact that as soon as I showed the two women my bruises and Mum knew I was going to be taken into care, she allowed her mask to slip, and finally someone outside the family was able to see her for what she really was – a foul-mouthed, screaming bully who was more than capable of inflicting physical violence on her daughter.

Before I left the house that day, the social worker checked my bag, and I can remember feeling embarrassed when I told her I didn't have a toothbrush. Although my brothers all had their own, I had to steal toothpaste from the cupboard in the kitchen and smear it on my finger to clean my teeth. It must have been obvious to Valerie Hampton that I was anxious, but instead of saying something comforting to try to make me feel better, she told me coldly, 'You will be given a toothbrush and tooth-paste when you arrive at the children's home. Any other toiletries you require will be purchased for you in due course.' So I didn't say anything else.

When we got downstairs, the social worker opened the living-room door and said, 'Say goodbye to your parents, Zoe,' which was something I hadn't even thought about doing and the prospect filled me with dread. But I needn't have worried, because Mum wasn't there. 'She doesn't want to talk to her,' Dad told the social worker. Then he handed me a £5 note and told me to be good, and I followed the social worker out of the house.

I was very frightened when I left home that day. However dysfunctional my family might have been and however unhappy I'd been throughout all the time I was living with them, it was the only home I'd ever known and I couldn't even begin to imagine what lay ahead. But as well as being frightened I was relieved, because whatever *did* lie in store for me, I knew it couldn't be as bad as spending the rest of my childhood being beaten by my mother and living in constant fear of being sexually abused by my dad.

It wasn't until I was sitting on the back seat of the social worker's car clutching my school bag that what she'd said about a children's home finally sank in and I asked her, 'Aren't I going to a foster home then?' The image I'd always had in my head of the 'better place' I might be able to live if I ever plucked up the courage to ask for help was of a clean house with sunny rooms that smelled of furniture polish, with foster parents who bore a striking resemblance to my friend Carly's mum and dad. So I was disappointed when she said, 'There isn't anyone available at the moment who can deal with ... Who can take you in.'

Perhaps the words she didn't say were 'someone with your issues of drinking and self-harming'. Then, after pausing for a moment, she told me, 'We've found a bed for you at a place called Denver House. It's a residential care home for children of your age. You'll be fine there for a few weeks, while we do the assessments we need to do.'

It wasn't what I'd been hoping for and I was disappointed not to be going to a foster home. But even being at Denver House was going to be better than being at home. Or so I thought.

Chapter 6

We were driving through town on the way to the children's home when the social worker suddenly said, 'Oh look, isn't that your mum?' She must have left the house almost as soon as we did and I could tell that the social worker was surprised to see her out shopping, carrying on as normal as if nothing had happened. I wished she hadn't pointed her out though, because I still believed that it was *my* fault Mum didn't love me, and my heart ached when I saw her.

It was late afternoon when we arrived at Denver House. My first impression was of a large, intimidating building that wasn't homely at all, in any way. In fact, a girl who came for a brief stay a few days later freaked out when she saw the bars on the office window, because she thought she was going to be locked in, like in a prison. It was an impression that Yvonne, the very stern woman who was in the office on the day I arrived, did little to dispel.

With her long, billowing skirt, 'sensible' flat-heeled shoes and a mouth that turned down at the corners, Yvonne looked as though she probably disapproved of smiling and never indulged in it herself, which was a first impression that proved to be very accurate. She was bad-tempered too, and got really angry with some lads who burst into the room to have a look at the new girl while she was explaining the rules to me. After she'd shooed them out and shut the door, I could hear them laughing and running up and down the corridor, until eventually she went out and shouted at them to be quiet because they were scaring me, which was true, although I think I was even more intimidated by her than I was by them.

When another woman came to take me to my room, I kept my head down as I followed her through what seemed to be a maze of corridors and up the stairs to the first floor. Each corridor was divided by a couple of glass fire doors and carpeted in a rough material that was more like something you'd wipe your feet on than actual carpet. 'That's your bathroom,' the woman said, nodding her head towards one of the four or five doors we passed before she stopped, unlocked another door and added, 'This is your room.' Then, after she'd searched my bag for anything I could use to harm myself – or someone else – she gave me a key, told me I'd be charged for a replacement if I lost it, and left me there alone.

Dismal as it was, my bedroom at home was almost luxurious compared to the stark austerity of the room I had at the unit. The furniture consisted of a narrow wardrobe, a small set of drawers and a bedside table, all of which was industrial grade, designed, like the carpet, to be hard-wearing rather than to look nice. There was a narrow fold-up bed too, the sort of thing you'd normally keep tucked away in a corner somewhere for use by an occasional visitor. In fact, the mattress was so thin it provided almost no protection from the metal springs of the bed frame, and after I'd slept on it for a few nights, a sympathetic member of staff gave me an extra duvet to put under the sheet. But at least there was a lock on the door.

I had to go down to the dining room at tea time, but because of the problems I have eating in front of other people, I sat on a sofa at one end of the room, as far away as I could get from where all the other kids and members of staff were sitting, and didn't eat anything at all that night.

Sensing that some of the kids were looking at me, I avoided making eye contact with any of them as I examined my surroundings. The carpet at my end of the room was the same dark green as the one in the corridors, and as well as another pink-cushioned cane sofa like the one I was sitting on, there was a bookcase with a few books, some board games and a half dozen copies of *National Geographic* magazine on its shelves. The floor at the other end of the room – the eating end – was covered in thick lino, which was separated from the carpet by a strip of metal, and as well as two dining tables – one for the staff and the other for the kids – there were some mismatched chairs that looked as if they'd probably come from charity shops.

We were allowed to watch TV in our rooms for a couple of hours every night, so after everyone else had finished their tea, I went back upstairs and watched *A Touch of Frost*, because it reminded me of being at home with my family, or at least of sitting in my bedroom and hearing the theme music playing when they watched it together downstairs.

Like the woman in the office when I arrived earlier that afternoon, the member of staff who came to take the TV away didn't smile at me or ask if I was okay. Apart from telling me her name was Frances and that she'd come to collect the television, she didn't speak to me at all; she just unplugged the set, picked it up and walked out of my room, leaving me to close the door behind her. In fact, I don't remember anyone saying anything nice to me on that first day. No one seemed to wonder how it might feel to be in a strange place full of people I didn't know, or to realise that just a few kind words might make it all a bit less daunting. Or maybe they just didn't care.

The sense I already had that nothing had been done to try to make Denver House seem homely and less like an institution was compounded when I was getting ready for bed and went to use the bathroom that I'd be sharing with the lads who had rooms on the same corridor. It wasn't that the bathroom was dirty; it was just old-fashioned and functional, like something you might find in a pub or a cheap hotel. There was no shower – we used a clear plastic jug to wash our hair; the bath and washbasin were a bit chipped, there were pink tiles on the walls, lino on the floor, and a sanitary bin that was emptied at regular intervals by someone from a sanitary waste disposal company.

I was in a really bad way by the time I went to live at Denver House. My confidence and self-esteem were low and I found it difficult to do even simple things like keep myself clean. So I was very anxious when told that I would be expected to have a bath every day in a shared bathroom. In fact though, the problem was easily solved when I discovered that the staff ticked things off on the daily record sheets whether you'd done them or not, after which I just splashed some water on my face in the basin instead, and no one seemed to bother.

The following morning, a member of staff showed me how to use one of the large washing machines that lined a wall in the laundry room. 'You will be responsible for washing your own clothes,' she told me. 'The staff here are not your servants.' They did wash the bedding, however, and after we'd stripped our beds every Saturday we had to take our sheet, pillowcase and duvet cover downstairs, then collect clean ones from the untidy pile that had been dumped in the cupboard where all the cleaning stuff was kept.

My mum always made my bed when I lived at home, which was one of the reasons why I wasn't ever allowed to sit on it. Fortunately, however, I'd learned how to do it myself just a couple of years earlier, during a school trip I'd been on to an activity centre, which lasted for five days and four nights and which I wished would never end. So at least I didn't have to embarrass myself at Denver House by asking how to change my bedding.

There were just five lads and one other girl living at Denver House when I arrived. I didn't see the girl much, and my first impression of the lads was that they were all quite wild, although maybe they were just used to the routine. What I also found intimidating during the first couple of days was that there seemed to be a lot of arguments between the kids and the staff, and a real sense of 'them and us', like there is between prisoners and prison officers in TV programmes. So even though no one was openly hostile or aggressive, I was quite scared of the other kids to begin with, although that changed to some extent the second night I was there.

After supper that evening, most of the lads went to the TV room and I decided to follow them. Of all the rooms in Denver House, the TV room was probably the most homely, even though the blue paint on the walls was scuffed and the dark-grey carpet too bristly to be comfortable to sit on. The furniture consisted of a TV on a stand, two sofas and a single armchair, which actually matched and could have come from Ikea, rather than being charity-shop rejects like most of the rest of the furniture in the building, but which had burn marks on the armrests that I found out later were caused by the habit several of the lads had of holding lighters to almost anything that was made of wood.

Opposite where I was standing in the doorway of the TV room, watching the boys messing about, there was another open door through which I could see into a room with pale-yellow walls and the same grey carpet that was only very slightly bigger than the pool table it contained. I was just leaning forward to get a better view into it when a boy who had said hello to me and seemed quite friendly the night before suddenly pushed me. I don't think it was personal. I think he was just trying to look big in front of the other lads. But I knew instinctively that if I didn't stick up for myself right from the start, I'd end up being bullied by everyone. So I pushed him back, and we started to fight.

Fortunately, after we'd wrestled each other to the ground, I managed to get on top of him and hit him on the head with my trainer, much to the amusement of the other boys, who were standing around us laughing. The whole thing probably only lasted a few seconds, but I'd been right to stand up for myself and no one else bothered me after that.

When I was quite young, my brother Ben got a punch bag, which he put up in one of the sheds in the garden at home. I had already seen boxing on the television and had been completely enthralled by it, because it was so quick and clever and because the men were sweating and I thought they were shining. So by the time I saw the *Rocky* films a bit later, I was already hooked.

I know some people hate the violence of boxing, but it does involve skills and sportsmanship that I found inspiring. And perhaps I was also struck by the whole concept of being able to fight back. So, as I wasn't allowed to touch my brother's punch bag, I'd made my own out of a 3-litre cola bottle that I filled with grit, then somehow managed to tie to a rafter with some washing line in the other, very rickety garden shed. I couldn't hit the bottle very hard – the grit-filled plastic would probably have broken my knuckles if I'd tried – but just going through the motions made me wonder if maybe *I* could fight back too, which I had actually done, just once, before my brief encounter at the unit.

It was at primary school and a couple of girls had asked me and my friend Martha to go to the park with them. But when we got there, they started hitting me and calling me names, then chased after me when I tried to run away. They had obviously planned it, and when Martha ran up a ladder on to the climbing frame and refused to come down to help me, I decided to try to talk to them.

'Why did you ask me to come to the park with you if you don't even like me?' I asked them.

'Because you're fat and ugly,' one of them said.

Then she kicked me, they both laughed, and I punched her in the face. I only did it once. I know it isn't okay to hit someone, and I *had* tried to talk to them. But I'd never experienced anything that came even close to the feeling of satisfaction I had knowing that I could stand up for myself and refuse to be bullied. It was their turn to run away after that, and the next time I saw them they were nice to me and we became friends. It was a lesson I put to good use that night at Denver House, and although I didn't ever become real friends with anyone there, most of the lads were actually all right.

It was possible to avoid having much contact with the other kids in the unit most of the time, except at meal times when we were all supposed to be in the dining room. Even that rule wasn't really enforced, however: if you weren't there, you simply didn't get anything to eat until the next meal. So I ended up hardly eating anything at all, although I don't think any of the staff even noticed. Certainly no one ever tried to talk to me about the issues I had with food. Eating your meals in the dining room was just another thing they ticked off on the daily record sheets whether you'd done it or not.

There's a saying 'First up, best dressed', which I think used to refer to children in large, poor families who had to share their clothes: the first child to get up in the morning could take their pick, while the last to surface would have to make do with whatever was left, even if it didn't fit. It was pretty much like that at Denver House too, with the charity bags of clothes people used to drop off for us, and with the bedding – for example, the last lad to collect his bed linen on a Saturday morning might end up with pink sheets. I suppose it didn't matter in the greater scheme of things that some of the stuff we were given was okay and some of it really wasn't. But it seemed to be yet another indication of the general lack of thought that was evident in lots of aspects of the way the staff at the unit treated us, which was a shame looking back on it, because for kids who already believe they're worthless, even small things can reinforce the idea that anything is good enough for them. It's obvious when you think about it, which no one at Denver House seemed to do at the time.

The good thing about the staff's indifference – or what seemed like a good thing to me at the time – was that it meant I was mostly left to do whatever I wanted to do, which, during the school summer holiday when I first went there, was pretty much nothing except lie on my bed staring at the Eminem posters on my walls and trying not to think.

I was – and still am – a huge Céline Dion fan. But when a member of staff heard me playing one of her songs in my room one day, she told me, 'You'd better not play that out loud if you want to fit in here.' So after that I used headphones, and got the Eminem posters, not because it was the sort of music I listened to, but because it was what the other kids liked.

Although complaining about rules is something teenagers are expected to do, it's surprising how scary it is when there are no boundaries at all, or at least none that anyone tries to enforce. So despite having wanted to get away from my family and have a different life, the fact that the kids at the unit drank, smoked – cigarettes and cannabis

– and sniffed solvents while the staff didn't seem to care when they broke the rules made me feel very anxious and unsafe. And perhaps if the curfew that was supposed to be in place had been enforced, I wouldn't have been subjected to the terrible things that happened while I was living at Denver House.

The other girl who was living there when I arrived was called Abbie. She was 15, but the thick make-up and clothes she wore – mostly tight trousers, low-cut tops and boots – made her look older. Tall, slim and quite good-looking, she seemed confident and sure of herself, and appeared to do pretty much whatever she wanted, including disappearing for days at a time, apparently without any of the staff knowing where she was or asking her any questions when she came back. The few times I saw her during the first couple of weeks she ignored me completely. I could see that the lads were wary of her too, because they behaved differently when she was there, giving her fags whenever she demanded them and doing whatever else she told them to do – 'Give me this. Fetch me that.' – without any hesitation.

You don't make friends in a place like that. You try to get on with people because you have to, and the best you can hope for is that no one actively tries to make your life miserable. So I suppose I was flattered when Abbie knocked on my bedroom door one evening after I'd been living there for about three weeks and asked if I wanted to go to a party with her.

I'd just got back from a miserably unsuccessful visit to see my parents, which I'd only agreed to go on because my social worker kept telling me I should go and see them so that I didn't lose contact with them. A member of staff had given me a pass for the bus to get there and back, but when I'd rung the bell, my mum had opened the front door and told me, 'You just don't get it, do you? We don't love you and we don't want you. I don't know why you've come.'

I found out later that she'd told my social worker that's how she felt, but I was still encouraged to go home. What really hurt on that occasion, however, was knowing that my father and brothers were in the house and must have heard what she said to me, and yet they didn't make any attempt to see me or say anything to me at all.

After Mum had shut the door in my face, I walked back to the bus stop in floods of tears, feeling rejected and utterly alone. So Abbie's invitation came at just the right moment, when I needed something to take me out of myself, and I can remember thinking, 'Don't blow this, Zoe. This might be your one chance to have a friend here.'

I was a bit worried in case my jeans, trainers, hooded jacket and the cap I'd started wearing all the time so that I didn't have to look people in the eye would make me look out of place at a party. But they were the only clothes I had, and as Abbie didn't seem bothered, I followed her down the stairs, out of the front door of Denver House and down the road to where a blue Ford Fiesta was parked with its engine running.

Chapter 7

'This is Zoe,' Abbie said as she opened the front passenger door of the car and got in, while I clambered into the back. I don't know how old I'd have expected her friends to be if I'd had time to think about it. Probably not as old as the three men in the car, who must have been at least twice our ages and, I felt, quite intimidating as I sat there with my shoulders hunched and my hands clasped tightly in my lap, trying to avoid making any physical contact with the man sitting next to me, and wishing I hadn't come.

The rundown terraced house they drove us to was just a few streets away from the unit, and there was no party going on when we got there. Which was a relief in one way, because it meant I didn't have to try to think of things to say to a bunch of self-assured people who would think I was stupid. In fact, I didn't have to think of anything to say to anyone, because the three men joked and talked to each other, and sometimes to Abbie, and only seemed to remember I was there at all when one of them refilled my glass with vodka or handed me a joint.

After a while, when the alcohol and cannabis had just started to dull my senses, the man who had told me his name was Yasir stood up and said, 'Come with me. I want to show you something.'

'Me?' I asked, looking up at him from where I was sitting on the floor leaning against a grimy sofa.

·'Yes, you.' He smiled at me. 'Come on. It's upstairs.'

Maybe my senses had been dulled even more than I'd realised, or maybe it was just the naivety of a 13-year-old schoolgirl that made me feel safe, if a bit awkward, with Abbie's friends and made me think as I followed Yasir up the stairs that he really was going to show me something.

'It's in here,' he said, opening one of the three closed doors on the landing. I could smell the damp as soon as he turned the handle. But it was only when I stepped inside the room and saw the bare floorboards and stained mattress that I realised I had made a mistake to trust this man I didn't know.

'I don't think ...' I said, taking a step backwards just before he grabbed me by the shoulders, pulled me inside the room and tried to kiss me. I was still more embarrassed than scared as I turned my head away, trying to avoid looking at him as I dodged his kiss. But I started to feel mildly anxious when he attempted to kiss me again, tightening his grip when I started to struggle, so that I couldn't break free. Then, suddenly, he twisted his fingers in my hair, yanked my head backwards and began to unbutton his trousers. That was when the fear took over and my whole body began to shake uncontrollably.

'Hey!' He held me away from him for a moment, without loosening his grip. 'It's okay. Don't worry. Just pretend I'm a doctor and I'm going to make you better.'

I don't think I could have guessed that the one person I would think about when I was really scared was the person I'd been most frightened of for as long as I could remember. But as the man forced me to my knees, I found myself praying silently, 'I need you now, Mum. Please, just love me enough to come and rescue me.' Then, with his fingers still grasping a clump of my hair, he pulled my head back again and tried to force his penis into my mouth. I was panicking and trying to turn away, but he was much stronger than I was and his grip was like a vice clamping my head so that I couldn't move.

'Imagine you're sucking a lollipop,' he said, his voice perfectly calm as if he was talking to an even younger child than me. 'You'll be all right – if you do as I say.'

'No – please – don't,' I pleaded with him. Then he pushed his penis into my mouth and some instinct told me that the only chance I had of keeping myself safe was by doing whatever he told me to do, even though the smell of sweat and urine was making me gag, and I was crying because what he was doing was so horrible and because I thought I was going to choke.

We'd had sex-education classes at school by that time, and I'd seen my dad doing things to my mum when they were both drunk and she was screaming 'No'. But I was just 13 years old and a virgin, and I didn't want to lose my virginity to *anyone*. So when he pushed me down on to the mattress and climbed on top of me so that his weight was crushing my chest and I couldn't breathe, I became almost hysterical. I was still sobbing and saying silently in my head, 'Please, Mum, help me,' when he reached down with one hand, undid the zip on my jeans, then pulled them down with my pants and raped me.

I thought he'd done what he wanted to do and it was all over when Abbie came into the room, laughed, then turned around and walked out again. But when I tried to get up and follow her, he pushed me back down on the mattress again and said, 'No. I haven't finished yet.'

A few minutes later, after he'd ejaculated inside me, he got up, stood in the light in the doorway, pulled a dirty handkerchief out of his pocket and wiped himself clean.

It was only when I sat up that I realised he'd removed the trainer from my left foot and taken my left leg out of my jeans and underwear, while leaving everything on the right side in place. I remember being surprised that I hadn't noticed him doing it. Then the pain kicked in as I tried to stand up, just as he said, coldly, 'Stay there,' then walked out of the room.

I was too scared not to do what he told me, but he hadn't said I couldn't get dressed, and I was just putting my left foot into my underwear when one of the other men came into the room. I knew what he was going to do even before he dug his bony fingers into my shoulders and forced me back on to the mattress. So I just lay there, rigid with shock and too exhausted to resist, while he pawed at me, because the damage had already been done, and as I was no longer a virgin, what would be the point of struggling and trying to protect myself now?

A few minutes later, after the second man had raped me and ejaculated inside me, he spoke to me for the first time since he'd come into the room, saying, 'Get dressed and come downstairs with me.' And because I didn't want to give him time to change his mind, I tried to ignore the searing pain that seemed to be shooting from my groin to the top of my head and quickly pulled on my pants and jeans.

When we went downstairs and into the living room, Abbie was having some kind of disagreement with Yasir, the first of the two men who'd raped me. They seemed to be arguing about some money she was insisting he owed her, and as I sat down on the floor beside the sofa again, as if nothing had happened, it dawned on me that the money she was demanding was for taking me to the 'party'.

In a way, understanding the role Abbie had played in what had just been done to me was almost as much of a shock as being raped had been, because it hadn't even crossed my mind that she might have betrayed me in that way. I don't know if she had sex with any of the men that night, although I'm sure she'd done so in the past, but I know she really believed they were her friends. So maybe she didn't realise that they were exploiting her just like she'd exploited me, and quite possibly other girls before and after me. What I haven't ever been able to understand is how she could do that to any other girl, even one she didn't know or care about.

She was still arguing with Yasir when the man who hadn't raped me handed me a glass of vodka and said, 'Drink that.' Maybe I looked as traumatised as I felt and he was trying to be 'nice', although that's difficult to believe in the context of what had just happened. Whatever the reason, I was grateful for the drink and for the very slight easing of the tension in my body as I felt it burning the back of my throat, cleansing some of the dirt and disgust that still threatened to choke me.

I was just swallowing the last mouthful of the vodka in my glass when Yasir handed Abbie some money, then phoned for a taxi to take us back to Denver House.

'Don't tell anyone about anything that happened tonight,' Abbie threatened as soon as we were sitting in the back of the taxi. 'Do you understand? If you breathe a word to any of the staff at the unit, there'll be really serious consequences.' And because I was as scared of her as I had been of the men, I agreed to do as she said.

It was about 2 a.m. when the taxi dropped us off outside. Although we could come and go pretty much as we pleased during the day, the door was always locked at night, so

Abbie rang the bell. It was a member of staff called Tess who let us in, a very short, slim woman in her late forties who had tightly curled blonde hair and an attitude that normally ranged from cold to indifferent, but who, instead of being angry and shouting at us as I'd expected her to do, responded good-humouredly to Abbie's cheerful banter.

The waking night office was at the end of the same first-floor corridor my room was on, and as I followed them down the corridor, through the first fire door, past the contact room and up the stairs, I heard Abbie tell Tess, 'I'm never going to drink with Zoe again. She just can't hold her liquor,' and Tess laughed, as if she'd said something really funny. They were still laughing and joking together when we reached the office, where I left them and walked on down the corridor, crying silent tears with every painful step.

When I'd closed the door of my room behind me, I leaned against it for a moment, feeling very frightened and lonely and wondering what to do. Then exhaustion suddenly overwhelmed me, so I took off my clothes and was just pulling on the pyjamas with pictures of teddy bears all over them when I realised I was bleeding.

I hadn't had many baths during the three weeks I'd been at the unit. For the first few days no one had given me a towel and I was too embarrassed to ask for one, although just the thought of being naked and vulnerable with so many people around – even in a locked bathroom – made me feel sick with anxiety. Now though, I wanted a bath even more than I wanted to sleep, so that I could wash away the blood and the stench of the men who'd raped me.

It seems ridiculous when I think about it now that my confidence was so low I almost didn't dare go to the waking night office and ask Tess if I could have a bath. But when I did go, she said, 'No. It's far too late.' So I went back to my room and was just turning the handle on the door when a wave of nausea swept over me and I knew I *couldn't* go to bed with blood on my legs and someone else's sweat and semen on my body.

'*Please* can I have a bath,' I asked Tess again when I went back to the office. 'You see, the thing is, I've just started my period and I'm in a real mess.'

'Well, give yourself a wipe in the sink then,' she said, sighing as she turned her back on me.

Upstairs again in my room, I cleaned myself up as well as I could using the flannel I'd been given when I arrived at the unit, sobbing because of what had just happened to me and because I had no one to turn to for help or even just a sympathetic word. I can remember wondering why no one ever seemed to realise that I had feelings just like they did, and that having to go to bed covered in blood would make me feel as though I really was less than nothing. Did Tess have a daughter, I wondered just before I fell asleep, and if she did, would she have told *her* to wipe the blood off her legs with a flannel and go to bed?

When I woke up a few hours later, my first thought was that I might be pregnant. So, as soon as I was dressed,

I found a member of staff and told her I needed the morning-after pill. I didn't explain what had happened – I was even more afraid of Abbie than I was of being pregnant – and after I'd shrugged in answer to the couple of questions she asked me, she shrugged too and said, 'We'll have to inform your social worker that you've had sex. And, of course, your parents will need to be told.'

At that moment, I think I wished more than I had ever done before that there was someone I could trust and confide in. It was horrible knowing that my first sexual encounter was going to be discussed by people who didn't care about me and who'd assume I had *chosen* to have sex at the age of 13. I felt dirty because of what had happened, and I hated the thought that everyone would think it was my fault, when the truth was that the only thing I was guilty of was naivety and being lonely enough to have believed that someone like Abbie would really take me to a party, where maybe I'd make some friends.

By the time my social worker, Valerie, came to the unit later that day, I was so upset I'd decided to risk Abbie's retribution and tell her what had really happened. I was crying and could feel my cheeks burning with humiliation as I described what the two men had done to me. But I felt a sense of relief too, knowing that whatever happened next was now the responsibility of an adult who would know what to do because it was her job to look after children like me.

'I told Abbie I wouldn't say anything,' I said, suddenly afraid again of the 'really serious consequences' she'd threatened if I breathed a word to anyone. I'd been staring at my feet while I spoke, and when Valerie didn't say anything for a few seconds, I looked up at her and saw, to my amazement, that she was smiling. 'Well, Zoe,' she said at last, 'you're never going to be satisfied now with what most girls your age would think was a normal relationship. No heavy petting for you from now on. You're only going to be happy with full sex.' Then she laughed.

For a moment, I couldn't make any sense of what she was saying. I remember thinking, 'She can't have listened to a word of what I've just told her. She wouldn't have said something like that if she had.' I think I was expecting her to say that what had happened to me was wrong, that I had been raped and she was going to have to report it to the police, because it's a crime to rape someone, and a crime to have sex with a 13-year-old child under any circumstances. It certainly never crossed my mind that she'd laugh and make a joke of it, even if I hadn't been so obviously distressed.

So hadn't she been listening? Had she listened but misunderstood? Or was I over-reacting to something that wasn't actually a big deal because it didn't matter what happened to kids like me? I was still asking myself those questions when my social worker started singing some lines of a song from the TV programme *South Park*, which the kids in Denver House used to watch:

Suck on my chocolate salty balls.
Stick 'em in your mouth and suck 'em.

The next day, Valerie Hampton took me to a family plan-
ning clinic, where I was given a morning-after pill, a bag
of condoms and a prescription for a contraceptive.

Everything that happened as a direct result of my plea
for help after having been raped seemed baffling and
surreal. Why was I given contraceptives, for example? I
was 13 years old. I hadn't wanted to have sex and I didn't
intend to have it again – ever. But the assumption seemed
to be that from now on sexual activity would be part of
my new life, like cleaning my teeth with a toothbrush.
That was just the way it was going to be. So the sole
responsibility of the people whose care I had been placed
in was to provide me with the means of not becoming
pregnant. Now the question that kept going through my
head was, had Mum been right all along and I deserved
everything bad that happened to me? The answer seemed
to be 'Yes'.

People sometimes talk about girls who are 'divas', who
behave as though the world revolves around them and
they deserve special treatment and the best of everything.
I've known girls like that myself and they *are* irritating.
But then there are girls like me, who are at the other end
of the spectrum and believe that they don't deserve
anything good at all. It's difficult to explain what that feels
like. One outcome of it is that you accept whatever's

thrown at you, particularly when you discover that summoning all your courage and telling someone you need help doesn't have any effect at all.

What was even more shocking than my social worker's reaction to what I'd told her was the response of another member of staff, who said, 'I knew something like that was going on.' She didn't say it in a tone of voice that suggested she was outraged or felt guilty for not having acted on her suspicions. In fact, she sounded almost triumphant for having been proved right. But even when they did have proof and knew that at least one of the girls in their care had been raped, they still did nothing.

Despite all the staff at the unit eventually knowing what had happened, not one of them ever spoke to me about it, suggested that I should talk to them if I had any concerns, or told me not to worry because in future they would make sure I was safe. What made it even worse was discovering that my teachers at school knew about it too, after it had been discussed at a review meeting attended by my head of year. So now everyone would think I was the 'slag' and 'slut' my brother Jake used to say I was long before I even knew what the words meant.

There *was* one thing I was certain about though: it wasn't ever going to happen again. So I started taking great care to avoid Abbie, and spent even more time alone in my room. Then, a few days after she had taken me to the 'party', she knocked on my door, and kept on knocking until I answered it.

'I haven't seen you for a few days,' Abbie said, picking up a book from the bedside table and flicking through its pages.

'I … I haven't been feeling very well,' I told her, hoping she wouldn't notice the tremble in my voice.

'Yeah, well, I've been out a lot.' She dropped the book on the bed. 'But, anyway, I thought you might like to meet some more of my friends.'

'No. No, thanks,' I said, trying to swallow the hard lump of anxiety that seemed to be stuck in my throat.

'What the fuck do you mean, "No, thanks"?' I recoiled instinctively as she bent down and spat the words into my face. 'Oh, I get it,' she said, standing upright again and smiling the way my mum used to do when something bad was about to happen to me. 'You thought I was asking. Like an invite. Well, I wasn't. And unless you want your fucking head kicked in, you better be ready to go in ten minutes.'

Anyone who hasn't ever had to do something they really, really didn't want to do probably can't imagine what it's like to have no choice. And although it might be true to say that, ultimately, everyone *does* have a choice about most things, sometimes the potential consequences make you feel as though you don't. That's how I felt that night when Abbie paused in the doorway as she was leaving my room and said again, 'Ten minutes.'

It was probably nearer eight minutes later when I walked out of Denver House with her and into a life that was more wretched and soul-destroying than any I could ever have imagined.

Chapter 8

It wasn't long before Abbie was arranging almost daily meetings for me, either with the men she called her friends or with taxi drivers. She knew a lot of taxi drivers. Sometimes they'd come on their own and sometimes there'd be one or even two other men with them when they picked us up almost outside Denver House. Mostly, they ignored me and spoke to each other in their own language. But they always gave me alcohol, either cider or vodka, which I soon learned to start drinking immediately so that the process of numbing my senses was well underway by the time we got to wherever we were going.

Usually, they would take me to a dismal, dirty house somewhere, or sometimes to a park with a secluded area where we wouldn't be seen. The houses were all very similar to each other and most of them didn't seem to be lived in; there would just be a room with a dirty mattress where the men would take me to have sex or to perform oral sex or masturbate them. Most of them hurt me, and usually there were at least two or three of them in every house who came to the room either separately or together.

I've blocked most of them out, but I can still remember some of them and the things they did to me. Like the man I pleaded with not to make me perform oral sex on him who took hold of my hair, pulled my head back until I thought my neck was going to snap and said, 'You will *not* like what I do to you if you don't do what I say.' Then he forced me on to my knees, thrust his penis into my mouth, and when I kept gagging and then started to choke, raped me instead, so brutally I couldn't find the alcohol-induced blank space inside my head that might have enabled me to block out what he was doing.

When the man finished, he told me impatiently to, 'Hurry up and put your clothes on,' then took me downstairs into the living room, where Abbie was sitting drinking with some other men, and said to her, 'You both need to leave now. I can't take you. You'll have to find your own way back.'

'Well, we'll need some *money*,' Abbie said, holding her hand out almost underneath his nose. But he swatted it away and said, 'Just go,' and as soon as we were outside she turned on me, saying angrily, 'It's *your* fault I didn't get any money. What did you do?'

'Nothing,' I answered, too ashamed and humiliated to tell her what had happened.

It was the early hours of a very cold morning and we were a few miles from Denver House, with no option other than to start walking. But we hadn't gone very far when Abbie stopped near a phone box, shoved some coins into my hand and said, 'Call them. Tell them we need a lift.'

'There's no one available to pick you up,' the member of staff who answered the phone told me. 'You've been reported missing to the police, so my advice would be to keep walking until you see a police car and flag it down or, failing that, until you get back to the unit.'

Abbie was even angrier with me when I told her what the woman had said, and after ranting and swearing at me for a while, we trudged along the road in silence.

We must have been walking for at least an hour when a police car drew up beside us. The officers didn't even ask where we'd been or what had happened to us. They just took us back to the unit, dropped us off on the road outside and drove away.

It was about 4 a.m. when we rang the bell, and I had school the next day. But when a member of staff woke me up at 7.30, I just couldn't face it and refused to go. If you stayed off school when you weren't ill, you were locked out of your room all day, and as all the recreational rooms were locked too, the only place you could go and sit was the dining room. So that's what I did, with members of staff waking me up every time I fell asleep and treating me as though I'd been out all night having a good time, even though they should have been able to tell just by looking at me that nothing could have been further from the truth.

I didn't ever want any of it to happen. I didn't want to have sex with any of the men and I never once went willingly to any of the places they took us. I did it because I was scared – of Abbie and of the men themselves – and because, having realised that the people who were supposed to be caring *for* me didn't actually care *about* me at all, I didn't have anyone else to turn to. The only thing that saved me during those weeks was the alcohol the men gave me. If I drank enough of it quickly enough, I could switch off – to some extent, at least. Otherwise, I don't know how I would have dealt with the horrible things that were done to me.

While all this was going on, I did go home a few times, because my social worker kept telling me how important it was for me to stay in contact and visit my parents. I didn't want to go at all – except perhaps to see my little brother – but she would say things like, 'I really do think it's a good idea, Zoe. You don't want to lose contact with your mum and the rest of your family, do you?' The honest answer to that question would probably have been 'Yes', certainly as far as Mum, Dad and Jake were concerned. But she made me feel as though my reluctance was an indication that there was something wrong with *me*, rather than a normal response to having been beaten, bullied and made a scapegoat of by my mother for as long as I could remember.

What made her insistence even more bizarre was the fact that the conclusion of the assessment that had been done – which was the reason I'd originally been taken into care for what was supposed to be just a few weeks – was that my parents were unfit to look after me. So it had been decided that I should remain in care until I was old enough to be independent – legally, if not practically or psychologically.

The visits usually ended badly. Mum was never happy to see me and sometimes wouldn't let me in, while Dad just leered and said horrible things to me that would have been creepy and disturbing even if he hadn't been my father. Then one day, when I was feeling particularly trapped and desperate at Denver House, I decided I'd had enough and that although I didn't *want* to go home, it was the only place I *could* go.

The house was about a 20-minute bus ride from the unit, although it seemed much longer on that occasion, and several times when it stopped at a bus stop I almost changed my mind and got off, until I thought about Abbie waiting for me back at Denver House. When I got there, Mum answered the door and when she saw me standing there crying, all she said was, 'What the fuck do *you* want?' She didn't actually slam it in my face though, so I followed her through the house and into the kitchen. My oldest brother, Jake, had left home by that time, but Ben and Michael were there, watching TV in the living room with Dad, who didn't speak to me at all when my brothers said hello.

'I'm really unhappy at Denver House,' I told Mum. 'It's horrible. Can I come home, Mum? Please.'

'It's not a fucking hotel,' she shouted at me, and even when I begged her, 'Please, Mum. I really can't live there anymore,' she just looked triumphant and said spitefully, 'Well, you should have thought of that before you showed those bitches your bruises, shouldn't you?' Then she told me to leave, and although Dad and my brothers could hear every word we were saying, they carried on watching TV and didn't even try to intervene.

The walk back to the bus stop that day was one of the loneliest walks of my life. If you'd asked me a few weeks earlier whether I would ever have wanted to live at home again, the answer would have been a very emphatic 'No'. Now though, I knew that there were even worse things in life than being beaten and disliked by your own mother. What I didn't know until some years later, however, was that my dad had been informed by social services that I was 'actively engaging in sexual relationships with adult Asian and black males'. I was heartbroken when I discovered he'd been told such a horrible lie, which made it sound as though I was doing it because I wanted to, as if it was *my* choice, with no mention of what I'd told my social worker about having been raped. It still breaks my heart to know that Dad never knew it wasn't my fault and that I didn't choose to have sex with all the disgusting, abusive men who exploited and eventually trafficked me.

I had gone to live at Denver House not long after the summer holidays started, and just before I went to school for the new term, Abbie left the unit and suddenly it all stopped. For the first few days after she'd gone, I kept thinking I'd wake up one morning and she'd be back. But when I eventually asked a member of staff if they knew where she was, I was told that she'd turned 16, 'So she isn't our problem anymore.' Which meant – although I hardly dared to believe it – that she wasn't *my* problem anymore either, and the whole nightmare was finally over.

You never really know why people do some of the things they do, and I don't know how Abbie got involved with those men or why, in effect, she sold me to them – apart from for the money they paid her, of course. She didn't seem to be frightened of them, so I don't think she'd been threatened or intimidated into getting me involved. Whatever her reason for doing it, however, I don't think I could have done that to another girl and I'm still very angry about it.

It was a huge relief after Abbie had gone to be able to go to school every day and sit in my room in the evenings knowing that she wasn't going to knock on my door and tell me, 'You've got ten minutes.' Then, about two weeks later, Natalie moved in.

Natalie was a larger, louder, more aggressive version of Abbie who also wore thick make-up and similar clothes, but had a much bigger personality in every respect. Also

15, she was involved with a lot of different men from the ones Abbie knew, and she scared me even more than Abbie had done. It was one thing hitting some girl in a playground who was bullying me, or wrestling a fairly puny boy to the floor to avoid being placed at the bottom of the pecking order that existed in Denver House. But I was actually a very timid little girl, and I knew when I'd met my match or, as was the case with Natalie, was completely out of my depth.

I'd almost stopped thinking for myself by that time anyway, and had found that if I drank enough alcohol, it masked the unnerving feeling I otherwise had that my soul had disappeared. So I barely even bothered to try to resist when Natalie told me one evening that she was going to take me with her to meet a friend. This time though, it turned out to be true, and although I was very wary of leaving the unit with her, the guy who was waiting for us in a car parked around the corner – who Natalie said was her boyfriend – did just drive us around while we smoked the cannabis and drank the alcohol he gave us.

We drove around with Pete a couple of times after that, drinking and listening to music. He was a quiet, brooding sort of guy, probably in his late twenties, who didn't ever really speak to me. In fact, he didn't say much to Natalie either, just mumbling something occasionally in response to the cheerful chatter she kept up almost without pause as she sat beside him in the passenger seat of his car.

Then, one day, Natalie told me Pete had a friend who wanted to meet me. 'It's all been arranged,' she said. 'Pete will pick us up tomorrow evening.'

I wanted to tell her I wasn't going to go, but after having seen her lose her temper with one of the boys at the unit, I didn't dare. I did tell my social worker though, and asked if she could help me. 'I'm scared of Natalie,' I confided in her. 'So can you stop it? Can you ground me or something so that I *can't* go?'

'I'll speak to the staff and see what I can do,' Valerie Hampton told me.

All the kids at the unit had 'issues' of some sort, and some of the boys would kick off from time to time. But their actions were tame compared to the hurling of tables across rooms and trashing of the building that were Natalie's responses to someone upsetting her or trying to stop her doing something she wanted to do. So I don't think it was just me and the other kids who were frightened of her. The staff seemed to be intimidated by her too, so I suppose it was easier for them to avoid antagonising her in the first place, rather than having to confront her about something and then deal with her reaction. Which I assume is why my social worker didn't do anything in response to what I'd asked her, or even mention it to me again.

In fact, the nearest anyone came to acknowledging what I'd said was another member of the staff who told me a few days later, 'You need to make your own choices, Zoe. It's up to you to decide what you do or don't do.' I did wonder, once again, if they hadn't understood what I'd said about being scared of Natalie or if they simply hadn't considered the fact that in order to be able to stand up to her and make my own choices, I would need to know that someone would be there to protect me when she retaliated, which they must have known as well as I did she would do.

When Pete met us outside the unit the following evening, he drove us to a house to meet his friend. No one told me the man's name, and I don't know if he actually lived in the house with the damp living room where we sat drinking for a while before he stood up and said, 'Come with me.'

He was a big man, at least 6 foot tall, and I was quite a small, very thin teenager. It wasn't just his height I found intimidating though. There was something about him I instinctively didn't like. But when I glanced at Natalie, hoping she'd see how anxious I was and tell me I didn't have to go, she just stared back at me coldly, as if daring me to refuse. So I got up and followed Pete's friend up the stairs to a bedroom, where he handed me another drink and started taking off his clothes.

I had just downed the glass of vodka he'd given me in one gulp when he said, 'Lie down.' And because I knew there wasn't any point in arguing, I lay on the filthy duvet, wondering if a time would ever come when I would be able to live through just one day without being afraid.

I could barely breathe when he climbed on top of me, because he was heavy and the weight of his body was pressing me into the thin mattress, and because the smell of his sweat was making me gag. Then, suddenly, he pushed my legs up behind my head, and a moment later I felt a sharp stab of pain.

'I'm too big for you,' he said, lowering my legs again before putting my hand on his penis and moving it up and down. When he ejaculated all over my fingers and my clothes, I thought I was going to be sick. But he was already cleaning himself up and pulling his stained T-shirt back over his head, so he didn't even notice that I was retching.

I hated every single soul-destroying sexual experience I ever had, and sometimes, as on that occasion, the man would be so repulsive that just the thought of his clammy skin touching mine made me feel as though I would never be clean again. What upsets me most about that particular occasion though – even today – is that for once I didn't try to stop him or say no, perhaps because I realised that, although Abbie had gone, nothing in *my* life was going to change.

Pete and Natalie had an argument in the car on the way back to Denver House that night, and when he suddenly swerved over to the side of the road and put his hands around her throat, I could see that she was as scared of him as I was. It was the early hours of the morning and when he dropped us off just down the road from the unit, we had to ring the bell – as I'd done many times before when I'd been with Abbie. This time, the door was opened by

Frances, the woman with the sort of orange-coloured skin that comes from spending too much time on a sun bed, who had come to collect the television from my room the night I'd moved in.

Earlier that day, a nice member of staff called Sue had been on duty and we'd all been messing around giving each other piggybacks. It was good when something like that happened, because everyone would be laughing and acting normally for a while, like you'd expect kids our age to do. Sue must have written something about it in the file that was always handed over to the night-time staff when they came on duty, and as soon as Natalie and I had stepped through the front door, Frances said jovially, 'What's all this I've been reading about piggybacks? I want one.'

What she should also have read in the file was that I had asked not to be allowed to go out that night. And yet there I was, ringing the doorbell at almost 2 o'clock in the morning, clearly having had a substantial amount to drink. What Frances didn't know was that I'd just had a prolonged session of sex with a man who was a stranger to me, who I found repulsive, and who hurt me, and that all I wanted to do was crawl into bed, close my eyes and not think about anything for the next five or six hours, until it was time to get up and go to school. So all I was said was, 'I can't give you a piggyback. I've had a drink and I might drop you.'

'I'll give you one.' Natalie's tone was as playful as Frances's had been.

'No. I want Zoe to do it,' Frances persisted. 'I want her to …'

'Well, if you don't want one from me, you can just fuck off,' Natalie shouted over her shoulder as she stormed up the stairs, kicking the panelling as she went.

So then I thought I had to do it. Fortunately, Frances was quite small, but it felt weird to be wearily jogging around the ground floor of Denver House in the early hours of the morning 'having fun' and I only managed it for a few minutes before telling her I couldn't carry her anymore.

Somehow, I'd lost the key to my bedroom door while I was out that evening, and when Frances came upstairs to open it for me, she insisted on giving *me* a piggyback down the corridor. I don't know why she did it. Perhaps she was just trying to show an interest in me, to make me feel that I had a friend. If so, it was a peculiar way of doing it, and after what had happened to me that night, it just made everything seem surreal, as if 'normal' was something that could change almost from minute to minute, depending on whatever some random person decided it should be.

Frances had taken me with her into town to get some shopping for the unit a few days after I'd moved in. I had seen her fly off the handle by that time and threaten some of the lads who were calling her names, so I knew she was quick to anger and hadn't wanted to go with her, but felt as though I didn't have any choice. She hadn't spoken to me at all during the 15-minute walk into town, most of which I spent trying to catch up with her as she marched on ahead of me. I didn't know why she was being so unfriendly, as if I'd done something wrong. So I was surprised when she said something nice to me a couple of days later. I can't remember what it was, just that it made me feel special, which I suppose is how I might have felt on the night of the piggybacks if I hadn't been so tired and distressed.

There were a lot of incidents involving Frances that occurred while I was living at Denver House that made me very confused about whether or not she liked me. Because there were quite a lot of staff members – three or four on duty during the day and three different people at night, one of whom always slept on the premises – it was difficult to get to know any of them, which I suppose is why I wasn't particularly bothered about winning the approval of most of them. Frances was different though, and I suppose it was at least partly because she bothered to take the time to talk to me that I developed a bit of a crush on her. The problem was, her attitude towards me varied significantly from time to time, for no reason that I could ever guess at.

If you went to your room in the evening when the staff asked you to, the night staff would come in a bit later with a big Tupperware box of biscuits. Like with the clothes and bedding, the first person they took it to could choose the best biscuits – usually chocolate Bourbons and Jaffa Cakes – while the last person had to make do with whatever plain, boring ones were left. One example of how nice Frances sometimes was to me was that when it was her turn to do the biscuit round she would tell me, 'I always come to you first.' Or she'd bring me a chocolate Kinder egg or a can of fizzy drink and say, 'I could get into trouble for doing this. I don't do it for anyone else, you know,' which made me feel special, because no one had ever paid me any attention or given me any treats before. Then, on other occasions, she'd say something nasty to me, or tell me she was going to leave Denver House to go and work somewhere else, then seemed to be pleased when I got upset.

I was drinking heavily at that time, saving the £3.50-a-week pocket money and £2 a day I was given for school dinners to buy bottles of strong, cheap cider called Frosty Jacks. Obviously I was too young to buy alcohol myself, so I would stand outside a local store and say, very politely, to someone, 'Excuse me. Would you mind going into the shop for me, please?' Sometimes I got it wrong, but I became quite good at picking the right people to ask, mostly young men or women who would come out of the shop a few minutes later and hand me my change together with a carrier bag containing a 3-litre bottle of cider.

On some nights, when Natalie wasn't around, I would sneak out of the unit with my bottle of cider and my CD player, climb up on to the roof and listen to Céline Dion songs. I was only really able to cry when I was listening to music, and I would sit there with tears streaming down my cheeks thinking about the life I'd had at home and about what was happening to me now. Even though they were very painful thoughts and I felt incredibly lonely, I used to listen to the words of a song like 'Where is the Love?', look up at the vast expanse of stars above my head and think, 'One day I will find someone who loves me and then everything will be different.'

Simplistic as it might sound, listening to those songs was what kept me going while I was at Denver House, because they made me believe that although I might never have a family of my own, I could eventually find someone who would make it possible for *me* to 'spread my wings and fly' and then the future could be very different from the present and the past.

Chapter 9

On one of the nights when Natalie arranged for us to meet a taxi driver outside the unit, he handed her a bottle of cider as we got into the car, then drove to a park where there were already four or five other taxis and at least ten men standing in a group beside them. Natalie had kept the cider bottle to herself, so I hadn't had a drink before we got there and I was very scared when one of the men tapped on the window and she told me to go with him.

'I don't want to,' I said. 'Please, Nat, don't make me go.' But she just looked at me steadily, her eyes dark with threat, and hissed, 'Just do what you're fucking told.'

As soon as I stepped out of the car, the man grabbed my hand and dragged me towards where the other men were standing watching us. Natalie was watching too, from inside the taxi where she couldn't hear me when I whispered again, 'Please, Natalie. I don't want to.'

As we were walking towards the men, they formed a circle on the grass and the man who'd grabbed my hand pushed me into the centre of it, where I was surrounded by a sea of grinning, leering faces. I can remember feeling as if I was trapped in a nightmare as I started turning around, searching for a way out. Then, suddenly, one of the men pushed me from behind, knocking the breath out of me and sending me sprawling on to the grass.

They were still all laughing as I got awkwardly to my feet. Then they started pushing me, their arms reaching out like tentacles to prod and poke me, and when one of them pulled down my trousers there was another ripple of laughter, which got louder and nastier when I reached down to pull them up and a different man yanked them down again, this time taking my underwear with them. I was crying by that time and while some of the men continued to grab at my body, others started pointing at me, saying things in a language I didn't understand that made everyone laugh even more.

The only slight reprieve I had as I stood there sobbing and trying to cover myself up was when someone pulled the bobble out of my hair and it fell across my face. I couldn't do anything to stop the men humiliating me, but at least I could no longer see them, and they couldn't see the shame that was burning my cheeks.

I don't know what would have happened if something hadn't spooked them, sending them all scuttling back to their cars. But suddenly Natalie and the taxi driver were standing beside me, telling me to put my clothes on and get in the car.

I was shaking as the taxi driver started the engine, and I felt grateful to Natalie when she handed me the bottle of cider he'd given her earlier. I was swallowing mouthfuls of it between sobbing breaths when I realised the taxi driver was looking at me in the rear-view mirror. Then he laughed and said something to Natalie about me having 'a jungle down there', which was a joke they both expanded on, between fits of laughter, as we drove back to the unit, while I concentrated on trying to drink as much of the cider as possible.

I hadn't drunk enough to stop me wanting to curl up on the back seat of the taxi and die when the driver suddenly turned round and snatched the bottle out of my hands, telling me, 'I don't think you deserve to drink this when my friends didn't get a chance to have fun with you.' Then he handed it to Natalie.

When we got out of the car outside Denver House, a young woman who had been coming out of the pub a few doors down ran up to me shouting something I couldn't understand and punched me in the face. I'd never seen her before, so I think she must have mistaken me for someone else, and as Natalie had run off as soon as she started shouting, I just told her I didn't want any trouble, then walked in the opposite direction, away from the unit, so that I didn't have to pass the crowd that was gathering outside the pub.

It was Frances who let me in again when I finally got back to Denver House and rang the bell. My eye was already swelling and starting to close, and my hair was all over the place, but instead of asking me what had happened, she sighed and said, 'I'm really disappointed in you, Zoe. It's only yourself you're letting down when you get into a fight.' Which really hurt, because by that time I cared a lot about what Frances thought of me.

It goes without saying that being raped and sexually abused has a terrible effect on you, both mentally and physically. But although it may not be on the same scale, being humiliated and made to feel like a piece of shit does too. And as I got into bed and pulled the duvet over my head that night, I felt even more desperately alone than I had done on every other night for as long as I could remember.

The next day, Natalie came to my room and gave me a razor, and after standing in the corridor outside the bathroom while I shaved off my pubic hair, she told me to unlock the door and let her in, so that she could check the evidence in the bath.

I sometimes felt like a mime artist while I was living at Denver House, trapped in a glass box that was invisible to everyone else but that seemed very real and inescapable to me. That was just my life though. I hated what was happening to me and I was very afraid that one day I would be taken to a house somewhere and wouldn't come back. It sounds ridiculous, I know, but despite sometimes seeing

Pete take money from the men who raped and abused me, I didn't realise until some time later that I was being sold.

I had sexual encounters with a lot of men in my town and elsewhere while I was being trafficked and controlled by Pete and Natalie. One man wanted me just to lie there while he masturbated over me, then pulled up my T-shirt and ejaculated on my stomach. Another told me to take off all my clothes and lie on the bed, then he lay down, naked, beside me, put his arms around me and touched my chest. Another forced himself inside me, then lay on top of me for a while without moving, before standing up abruptly and walking out of the room. And there were hundreds more, some of whom I remember and many that I don't.

One evening, Natalie took me on the bus to a house she said belonged to some friends of hers, who turned out to be two men in their thirties in a house that was just like all the others I'd been to. After we'd had a drink, Natalie went upstairs with one of them, while the other, who said his name was Jayden, came and sat next to me on the sofa and handed me the joint he was smoking. I knew what I had to do by that time, and although I knew, too, that there was no point fighting it, I pulled away when he tried to kiss me, then turned my head to one side when he pushed me back on to the sofa and tried again. I didn't struggle when he undid my jeans though, or when he took off his trousers, climbed on top of me, then spat on his hand and rubbed it between my legs. Even when I could feel the bile rising into my throat, I just lay there as he pushed himself inside me, praying that it would soon be over.

He had just finished when Natalie came back into the room with the other man, who told us, 'Jayden and me have got to go and pick something up. You stay here.' Then they walked out of the house, locking the front door behind them, which didn't seem to bother Natalie at all, and she called me a baby when I started to get upset. They did come back though, with a bottle of vodka, and after we'd had a glass of it, Natalie said, 'We've got to go. But we'll be back for the party tomorrow.'

Natalie went straight to her room when we got back to Denver House, but when I saw that my key worker, Susie, was on shift, I decided to tell her what had happened in the hope that she would do something to prevent me having to return to the house the following evening.

I liked Susie and I think she liked me too, particularly after the day when I was passing the dining room and heard some of the lads calling her names. She had brown eyes, shiny black hair and quite dark skin, which I suppose is why they were calling her 'Paki', and when I saw that she was very close to tears, I went in and said I'd lost the key to my room, just to give her an excuse to escape. I waited until we were around the corner and halfway down the corridor before I told her that I hadn't lost my key, and when I asked if she was okay, she burst into tears, thanked me, and gave me a hug.

'Can you remember where the house was?' Susie asked me on the evening when I explained about not wanting to go to the party. And when I said that I could, she drove me there and made a note of the address. 'Finally,' I thought, just before I fell asleep that night. But, once again, nothing was said about it the next day and no attempt was made to stop us going back there.

When I arrived for the party with Natalie the following evening, the house was full of men drinking and smoking cannabis. She went upstairs with the same man she'd been with the night before, and I was sitting in the living room dreading what was about to happen when the police arrived.

'I don't want to be here,' I told one of the officers, only daring to say anything because I knew Natalie was out of earshot. 'I'm 13 and I'm here against my will.' I was still scared in case one of the men heard me, but I knew the police officers would make sure I was safe. So I was shocked when one of them patted my shoulder and said, 'Come along now, you don't want to get these nice men into trouble, do you?' Then his colleague brought Natalie downstairs and they drove us back to Denver House.

I was still occasionally going home to visit my family. Sometimes, Mum let me in then ignored me, which was a bit depressing but better than being shouted and sworn at, or beaten up, which she also still did. In fact, she batted me so badly one day that Dad had to call the police, who came and took me back to the unit. Even then, the staff kept saying, 'You should go and visit your mum and dad.' So I'd try again, and tell myself that at least I had *somewhere* to go and a connection with the outside world. It didn't make anything better though, and on one of my visits I stole a bottle containing about a dozen paracetamol from the cupboard in the bathroom and took it back to the unit.

I didn't know how many would be enough to kill me, and I *did* want to kill myself; it wasn't a cry for help. Long before I went to live at Denver House, I'd seen suicide as the ultimate way out and assumed I'd have put an end to it all by the time I was 16. I'd often thought about doing it when I was being bullied and controlled by Abbie, and now that it had all started again with Natalie, it really did seem to be the only way out; the only way I could take back some control instead of worrying every time, 'Will this be the night that something happens to me? Will this be the night when I don't return to the unit?'

Some previous inmate of the room I was in at Denver House had made a hole in the wall, which someone had repaired with a bit of wood. But the nails were very loose and it was easy to remove it, which I sometimes did when the lad in the room next to mine tapped on the wall and offered to share a cigarette or joint with me. Remembering things like that makes me really sad, because it was such a normal 'kid thing' to do and it reminds me that that's what we were, just kids who wanted to do all the normal stuff but weren't allowed to because we had issues and our behaviour had to be monitored and controlled.

It was the lad in the room next door who put his hand through the hole and loosened the bit of wood that night. I think he was just going to say hello, until he saw that I was crying and holding an empty paracetamol bottle and asked me, 'Have you done something, Zoe? Have you taken some pills?'

When I shook my head, he asked me again, 'You have, haven't you? How many did you take? What's wrong?'

'Everything's wrong,' I told him. 'And yes, I did take some tablets. I just want it all to stop.'

I can't remember what happened after that, but he must have gone downstairs and told a member of staff, and a few minutes later someone came to have a look at me, to see if I was in imminent danger or could wait until after the handover from day-time to night-time staff. And I must have been okay, because it was about half an hour later when Frances came into my room and said, without any trace of sympathy, 'I've been told I need to take you to hospital.'

She didn't speak to me again until we were almost there, when she suddenly stopped the car and started banging her fists on the steering wheel saying, 'I don't know why you've done this, Zoe. It's something to do with me, isn't it? You've been funny with me for a few days, although I've no idea why.'

'It's not because of you,' I said. 'It doesn't have anything to do with you. It's because of … It's lots of things, to do with my parents and what was happening with Abbie and now with Natalie. And the reason I've been funny with you, as you call it, is because of what you said about me the other day in front of another member of staff.'

It had been the first time I'd felt really angry with Frances, rather than anxious and guilty because I thought I must be doing things that upset her. It was in the evening and Natalie was in my room when Frances suddenly burst in with another woman and said, 'Phew, Zoe, your feet smell.' Then all three of them had started laughing and making jokes at my expense, which had really upset me and humiliated me.

'Oh yes. I did do that, didn't I?' Frances laughed again at the recollection, apparently oblivious, or indifferent, to the fact that she'd hurt my feelings and distressed me. Then we continued our journey to the hospital, where I was kept in overnight, before being picked up the next morning by another member of staff and taken back to Denver House, where Natalie was waiting for me.

I didn't ever seriously consider not going with Natalie and Pete. None of the staff at the unit had taken any notice when I asked for help, and as I didn't have anyone else to turn to, I didn't seem to have any alternative when Natalie said, 'We're going out.'

We would sit on the low brick wall around the corner from Denver House almost every evening, waiting for Pete or a taxi driver to pick us up. Sometimes, Pete came with a friend, although usually he came alone, and Natalie would sit in the front passenger seat, chattering away to him cheerfully, while I sat in the back, trying to switch off and telling myself, 'It's just something I have to do. It doesn't matter.'

There's a time in the evening when people put lights on in their living rooms before they've drawn their curtains, and as we drove through unfamiliar streets, I would often catch a glimpse through a window into a cosy-looking room and wonder what it must feel like to be going home to a house like that, where someone who loved you was waiting for you.

When we arrived at whatever house we were going to that night, someone would give me a drink, and because I knew I wouldn't care so much when it kicked in, I'd drink it as quickly as possible, hoping it would start to take effect before the first man told me to follow him up the stairs.

After a while, Pete gave me a mobile phone, then started phoning me in the morning sometimes to say, 'Don't go in to school today. I'll pick you up in 20 minutes.' That's when he began to take me further afield, down the motorway to other towns, where other men abused me in other houses. I had always been frightened, but the fear got worse after that, and I believed that it really was just a matter of time before I went with him one day and didn't come back.

I had started Year 9 just after I'd been taken into care, but I missed a lot of school that year. I did try to do enough work to get by, because school was my only anchor and I wanted to stay on and do GCSEs. But I had already started to lose touch with my friends when I began to drink and take time off, and I think some of them judged me differently after I went to live in the children's home. Being a kid in care seems to create a barrier between you and the 'normal' kids, and even some of the friends who knew me before seemed to think I must be a thief or had done something else to warrant being 'put in a home'.

Sometimes, I'd stay behind after school to talk to one of my teachers, which was a bit sad really, because you'd hope to have 'better' things to do at 13 and 14 than hang around at the end of the day with a teacher. I didn't ever tell the teacher anything about the bad stuff that was happening; it was just nice to have someone to chat to. I think she must have known about some of it though, because there was always a teacher at the review meetings that were held with my key worker, my social worker and a really nice woman from the NSPCC called Mandy. My GP was invited to the meetings too, although I don't think he ever went, and so were my parents – Dad went a couple of times, but Mum never did.

Even my nan turned up at a meeting one day, which I was going to go to myself until I saw her standing in the doorway and fled. Apparently, they let her stay, which they shouldn't have done because it had nothing to do with her at all, but she could be very determined and stubborn, so maybe she just refused to leave. In the end, I think I only ever went to one meeting. I'd already told my social worker and the staff at Denver House what was happening, so I couldn't see the point of sitting there listening to them talking *about* me, never *to* me, knowing that nobody was going to do anything to help me anyway.

Mandy was different though, and she did get me some counselling in the end. But because horrible things were happening to me every week, it wasn't possible for the counsellor to keep pace with it all so that she could work with me on a specific problem. What those counselling sessions did make me realise, however, was that if I'd been put somewhere else, somewhere better than Denver House where I'd been given the support I so desperately needed from people like Mandy, who actually cared about kids like me, things might have been very different for me – then and now.

Chapter 10

When I went out with Natalie, I used to leave notes in my room at the unit saying things like, 'If I don't come back, this is the address of the house we're being taken to'. Or I'd write down Pete's phone number, or the number of one of the other men who used to text me to tell me what time they were going to pick me up. I know that at least some of those notes were found and read by members of staff, because they would have disappeared by the time I got back.

If we hadn't come back to the unit by midnight – which happened regularly – the staff would report us missing. Then, having done what they were required to do, we were no longer their responsibility and they seemed to forget about us. But the police only came to find us a couple of times.

On one occasion, a police officer found me in a car with a man who must have been twice my age. He shone his torch on my private parts as I was frantically struggling to pull up my underwear, but he didn't speak to me at all; he just told the man to take me home and then left. His attitude seemed to be that I wasn't like *his* daughters or the daughters of any of his friends, and that what I was doing in a car parked on a dark street was only what you'd expect from 'a care kid' like me. It was an attitude that was apparently shared by all the other police officers I encountered while I was in care. They'd probably act differently now – even though they might think the same way – but there wasn't the awareness 16 or 17 years ago, when I was a young teenager.

No one can ever really know how they'd react in a hypothetical situation: you might think you'd do one thing and then do something completely different when it actually happened. What I am certain about, however, is that if I'd had the help and support I should have had from the staff at Denver House, Abbie and Natalie wouldn't have been able to bully me and my life wouldn't have been destroyed by being trafficked and sexually abused. Unfortunately, the staff seemed to share the police's opinion that we were going to behave in certain ways and just needed to be contained – and restrained when necessary – until we were 16 and no longer their problem.

Some of the kids at the unit were quite often physically restrained, although not always for doing things that seemed to deserve it. I was more timid than most of the others and didn't ever kick off the way some of them did, but even I was restrained a few times too, for being upset rather than aggressive or violent. One day, for example, I was told that there was a phone call for me in the office and when I picked up the receiver, Mum said, 'Michael has something he wants to say to you.' I could hear some muffled sounds, like someone speaking with their hand over the receiver, then my little brother said, 'We don't want to see you anymore. We don't want you to come home again.' The line went dead before I had a chance to say anything, and although Michael was only eight or nine at the time, so I knew he wouldn't have thought of saying anything like that himself and that Mum must have put him up to it, I was still devastated and burst into tears.

Letting other people see you when you were crying and vulnerable wasn't a good idea at Denver House. I was bullied a bit by some of the other kids while I was there, and although it was never anything serious, I knew it would increase if I ever showed any kind of weakness. Which was another reason why all I wanted to do when the phone line went dead was get out of the office and up to my room, where I could cry with my face in my pillow so that no one could hear me.

Even though it must have been obvious to the members of staff who were in the office while I was on the phone that something had been said to upset me, instead of asking me if I was all right or just letting me go up to my room and hide until I might want to talk about it, someone shouted, 'Don't let her go.' And as I was running towards the door, another member of staff grabbed me and pinned me to the ground.

It was a totally unnecessary and disproportionate response to the situation, and the sort of thing that happened a lot at Denver House. Instead of being sympathetic and realising that I was likely to feel embarrassed about crying in front of other people, they made it seem as though *I* had done something wrong and needed to be restrained. So although they did manage to calm me down and then tried to talk to me, I could understand why some of the other kids reacted more aggressively to that sort of thing, because it isn't a huge step from being upset to being angry.

That phone call was typical of Mum. She was always thinking up new ways of being nasty to me, and getting my little brother, who she knew I loved, to say what he said was one of her more successful attempts. It wasn't just because it was Michael that had said it that upset me though; despite the fact that my occasional visits home were always miserable and sometimes very distressing, at least I'd somewhere to go, and a family – until now.

I'm sure every kid who ever stayed at Denver House could be a pain sometimes. The other thing we all had in common was that the problems that put us there weren't originally our fault, although we probably all thought they were, and perhaps the staff did too. For me, there were certainly some occasions when I would have benefited from being able to talk to someone with more understanding and less tendency to overreact than most members of staff seemed to have.

One of the other times I got into what seemed to be a disproportionate amount of trouble was after I'd got up a bit late one day and found that I'd missed breakfast. The rule was that if you missed a meal, you didn't get anything to eat until the next one, which was reasonable enough, I suppose, because otherwise there would have been kids asking for food 24 hours a day. They used to leave out a bowl of fruit and some juice, but I'd seen some of the kids spit in them. So, because I was very hungry, I sat on the floor in the doorway between the kitchen and the dining room and demanded some toast. I wasn't shouting or anything. I just kept saying, 'I'm not moving until you give me some.' Then the cleaners said they wanted to close the door and wouldn't clean the kitchen with me sitting there, and a few minutes later, two managers appeared, lifted me up by my arms and dragged me through the building to the contact room, which was used for meetings and reviews.

I had just been acting out like any teenager might do, but they hurt me when they manhandled me, and as soon as they let go of me, I tried to climb out of the window. I saw a report later that said a member of staff had 'tried to restrain me', whereas what she actually did was grab hold of my hair and yank me backwards into the room.

A lot of what the other kids did wasn't really bad either. It was just the sort of thing you'd expect from kids in that situation. Like breaking the lock on a shutter to get some food, for example, which was another incident I was involved in, this time with two partners in crime, one of whom was the lad I'd had a brief fight with when I first arrived at the unit, who was only 12 and didn't normally get into any real trouble. Again, it wasn't a terrible crime in the greater scheme of things. We were hungry, all the food was locked away, and we did something stupid to try to get something to eat.

After we'd broken the shutter, the three of us managed to hold the door to the dining room closed while a couple of members of staff were trying to force it open. Then we ran outside through another door, followed by a woman called Yvonne, who was the very stern lady who'd been in the office on the day I arrived at the unit. I'd subsequently discovered that she was someone who, although quick to tell everyone she was a devout Christian, didn't seem to think it was necessary to practise what she preached.

When she came running out after us, Yvonne managed to corner the young lad, who was obviously quite scared because he knew he was going to get into trouble. He didn't *do* anything though, other than stand there shouting. I can't remember what he was saying, but it was just kid stuff. But suddenly, Yvonne started screaming, 'Get off me! Get off me!' So then another member of staff, a guy called Des, came running out and told Yvonne to go to the office and calm herself down.

Always dressed in jeans and a polo shirt with gel-spiked hair, Des did look a bit younger than his age, which was probably mid-forties. In fact, he'd been a kitchen fitter before he started working with disturbed children at Denver House, although you'd have thought he had a degree in psychology the way he used to go on about things like Freud's belief that the human psyche could be divided into the id, the ego and the super-ego, which all developed at different stages in our lives and blah, blah, blah …

'He didn't do anything to her,' I told Des. 'He didn't touch her. He was just shouting.'

'Thank you, Zoe,' he said, in a tone of voice that made it clear he wasn't really thanking me, he was telling me to shut up, which was confirmed when he added, 'If I need your help, I'll ask for it.'

So I went inside and looked through the keyhole on the office door, then ran back down the corridor and told Des, 'You've got to come and look at this. She's scratching herself and making marks on her shoulders.'

I don't know if I expected him to believe me, but he did come inside and she was still doing it when he opened the door, then turned quickly to me and said, 'Okay, Zoe. Leave it now. I'll deal with it.'

Normally, they'd have called the police after an incident like that – three kids kicking off and smashing a lock on a shutter to steal some food. But on that occasion they didn't. Des just went into the office and closed the door, and no one said anything more about it.

I don't think Yvonne ever knew about the role I'd played in exposing what looked as though it was an attempt to claim that the lad had scratched her when she cornered him. I wouldn't have been able to tell from her attitude towards me anyway, because she'd already made it clear on many occasions that she didn't like me. Then, shortly after the lock-breaking incident, she became Natalie's key worker, and from then on she was all about Natalie.

It was at around the same time that a girl called Debbie came to live at Denver House. She was probably a bit younger than me, and even more withdrawn and anxious looking, and when I saw Natalie bullying her one day, I felt really sorry for her. The door was open as I was passing Natalie's room and I could see Debbie crawling around on her hands on knees, picking up dirty clothes and other stuff from the floor while Natalie snarled instructions at her.

Even though the kids often fought amongst themselves, no one would risk breaking the unspoken code and grassing on another kid. But Natalie was being really aggressive and Debbie looked terrified, and because I knew what it was like to be intimidated by her, I told a member of staff what I'd seen. Then obviously it got back to Yvonne, as Natalie's key worker, and a few of days later, when we were all sitting in the dining room, I heard her tell Natalie, 'You have to be careful, you know. You just don't know who you can trust in here.' She was looking at me as she said it, and I started to panic, thinking, 'She's going to get me battered.'

Fortunately though, Natalie didn't seem to notice, so I didn't get beaten up, as I know I would have done if she'd happened to look up from her plate and see the way Yvonne was staring very pointedly at me as she spoke.

Not long after that, Yvonne took us both into town to get what was referred to as 'personal needs' – toothpaste or sanitary pads or something similar – and while we were out she bought Natalie a Cadbury Creme Egg. It was a deliberately mean thing to do, and when I asked if I could have one too, she just shrugged and said, in a very un-Christian way, 'No. You're not my key child.' So I stole one and slipped it in my pocket without anyone noticing.

That was about as bad as I got really – just doing daft little things like demanding toast and stealing a Creme Egg. Even so, I ended up spending a night in a police cell on a couple of occasions, which was also totally out of perspective with what I'd done.

I don't know what triggered my reaction the first time. Something had happened that upset me and I ended up locking myself in the toilet upstairs and kicking off the loo seat. Earlier that day, I had volunteered to decorate the notice board that hung on the wall outside the office, using some wrapping paper that had been bought by a member of staff. I took a lot of trouble over it and it looked really nice by the time I'd finished. But when whatever it was that upset me happened in the evening, I got angry and ripped it all down again, then ran upstairs and locked myself in the toilet.

Tearing wrapping paper off a notice board and kicking a toilet seat didn't really amount to the crime of the century. But Yvonne was on duty that day and she called the police, and when I eventually came out of the toilet, she told me, 'We're going to send you to a different home, one for kids who are really violent and have loads of criminal convictions. That's the sort of place *you* ought to be living in.' Then the police arrived and I was put in handcuffs and taken to the police station, where I was locked in a cell for the night, which is a very scary experience for a 13-year-old.

When I was sitting in the back of the police car, the officer who'd arrested me turned around in his seat and asked, 'How long have you lived at Denver House?'

'Almost a year,' I told him.

'Bloody hell,' he said, with what seemed to be a genuine expression of surprise. 'You've done well to live in a children's home for almost a year and not to have been arrested before.' Then he laughed and turned away again, and I could feel my cheeks burning with shame.

After I'd been interviewed the next morning, I was given a caution, which is apparently classed as a conviction because it involves an admission of guilt. So although the caution itself only lasts for five years, it stays on your record for life and shows up if you ever have a Criminal Records Bureau (CRB) check, as I did some years later. I suppose they thought they were teaching me a lesson – which they did, although maybe not the one they intended to teach me. But can you imagine what would happen if every child in the country who ever did the equivalent of kicking off a toilet seat ended up spending a night in a cell and then being given a caution? The cells would be full and the police wouldn't have time to do anything else. Which would be good news for serious criminals, I suppose.

The other time I spent the night in a police cell was when I'd gone with some of the lads into a derelict pub down the road from the unit. We didn't even have to break a window to get in, and as the pub had been empty for years, anything that might have been left in it that was of any value had already been taken or smashed and destroyed, so we didn't do any damage or steal anything. We were just messing about behind the bar, pretending to serve each other drinks from broken beer pumps, when the police arrived.

Someone must have seen us climbing in through what remained of the window and phoned them, and I suppose we *were* trespassing. Once again though, there was no major crime being committed. In fact, we were more at risk from broken floorboards and falling masonry than the dilapidated building was from us. But you'd have thought we were doing something terrible judging from the reaction of the police officers – who arrived in four police cars.

What was really ironic when I think about it now was the fact that some kids messing around in an abandoned pub elicited such a swift, censorious response from officers working for the same police force that had repeatedly failed to act on information that a little girl hadn't returned to a children's home by the early hours of the morning and could probably be found at an address she had included in a note left in her room saying, 'If I don't come back, this is where I'm being taken. I don't want to go. I don't want to be abused by these men'.

Like many kids who end up in residential children's homes or with foster parents, I had been taken into care because of what someone had done to me – in my case, because of severe bruising resulting from my mother's regular beatings. It wasn't that *I* had done anything bad or had behaved in any way that indicated I needed to be professionally contained and restrained. To the police who came to the pub that day, however, we were, once again, simply 'care kids' who were doing what a lot of people would have expected us to do – causing trouble.

I didn't argue or strike any kind of attitude when I was arrested. I knew we shouldn't have been in the pub, so I wasn't angry or resentful when we got caught. I just cried, then got even more upset when one of the two officers who were driving me to the police station said I'd be spending the night in a cell.

'But I've got school tomorrow,' I told him. 'I want to go to school.'

'Well, I suppose you've got a choice then,' he said, looking at me in his rear-view mirror. 'We can either take you down to the station where you can spend the night in a cell and miss school tomorrow, or you can give me a blow job, then we'll take you back to Denver House and you can get up bright and early in the morning and go to school.'

I didn't know whether he was serious, although he seemed to be, but they both laughed when I said, 'I choose the cell,' which made me feel even more angry and humiliated.

When we got to the police station, I was charged with burglary with intent to steal, even though we hadn't had any intention of taking anything and, in any case, there was nothing there to take. Then I was locked in a cell and left there until about 4 o'clock the following afternoon, when I was given a warning, which was another black mark that turned up on my CRB check a few years later.

I did try to keep out of trouble, but no one seemed to take me seriously when I attempted to do anything to help myself. Even when I asked if I could join the local library, a member of staff burst out laughing as if the idea of a 'care kid' wanting to read a book was ludicrous. But books had been the only thing I'd had during all the solitary hours I used to sit in my bedroom at home, and I missed reading. So I kept on asking until eventually someone took me down to the library and provided the confirmation of my address that enabled me to join and take out some books.

Apart from the regular staff at Denver House, there were people who only came in when someone was needed to cover a shift, and one day one of them asked if she could borrow a library book I'd just finished reading. Which would have been fine if she had ever worked at the unit again while I was there; but she didn't, so I didn't get the book back. When I told a member of staff what had happened and said, 'I can't afford to buy a copy of the book and, anyway, it isn't fair that I should have to pay for it when it was a member of staff who took it,' she sounded impatient, as if I was being unreasonable, when she answered, 'Well, *you* wanted to join the library, and any books that are taken out on your library card are your responsibility.' I knew I wasn't being unreasonable though, and I was fed up of always being in the wrong. So I decided they could stick their library card and I wouldn't go there anymore, which really just meant I'd shot myself in the foot.

When I look back on it now, it's clear that even when I wanted to do something that any rational, caring person would have encouraged me to do, nobody tried to help me. In fact, sometimes, like when I said I wanted to join the library, they sneered at me, then acted as if it was *my* fault when an adult did something that made it all go wrong. They didn't ask the questions they should have asked either. For example, when Pete gave me a phone so that he could contact me when Natalie wasn't around and I gave the number to some of the staff at the unit, and to my family, no one asked the blindingly obvious question: how has a 13-year-old girl in care, with no access to money, suddenly got her own mobile phone?

I wanted them to have the phone number for the same reason I used to leave notes of car registration numbers in my room – because I thought it might help them to find me if, or when, I disappeared. Maybe it wouldn't have done, but at least I felt as though I had some sort of link with people who knew me when I was in a house some-where being sexually abused by men who wouldn't have been able to pick me out of a line-up of girls just ten minutes later.

There was no phone in our house, not that my parents would ever have phoned me if there had been, even before Mum got Michael to tell me they didn't want anything to do with me anymore. But my brother Ben – who was 21 when I turned 14 while living at the children's home – had his own mobile phone, so I did sometimes get texts, and very occasionally calls, from him, although he never said anything nice.

For example, I'd get a text out of the blue saying some-thing like, 'Mum said there's something up with you. Why are you doing this? What's wrong with you?' I knew he was referring to the fact that I was having sex with men all over the place, which Mum told him – and everyone else – I was doing because I wanted to. And although that was my social worker's fault for having told my parents it was my choice, I did tell them myself many times that it wasn't true and that I was being bullied into doing horrible things nobody would ever do willingly.

I didn't have any money to make calls or send texts on

the mobile phone Pete had given me, but we were occasionally allowed to make calls to our families from the phone in the office at Denver House, and sometimes I'd speak to Ben. Then, one day, when I was feeling lonely and miserable and phoned him just to say hello, he told me, 'Listen, Zoe. Don't contact me again. I can't deal with this.'

I was devastated. Despite teasing and sometimes bullying me when I lived at home, Ben was the only person who had ever cared enough about me to do things like take me into town when I was little to get my hair cut and buy me clothes. I couldn't bear the thought that he believed the stories he was told about me having 'loads of Asian boyfriends' and that, as Mum always claimed, I was the sole cause of stress for her – as if she would ever have cared what I did as long as I didn't live at home.

Frances – the member of staff who was sometimes nice to me – was in the office that day when I rang Ben, and when I dropped the phone and started sobbing, she picked it up, which is when he apparently told her, 'Don't let Zoe phone me again.'

I'd had a vast number of horrible experiences by the time I was 14, many of which I still struggle to come to terms with today and that I know will leave their mark on me for the rest of my life. My brother Ben saying that he didn't ever want me to contact him again was one of the worst, because although my spirit was crushed by the brutal violence of the men who sexually abused me, they were strangers who had no reason to care about me. Whereas Ben was my brother; he had lived in the same house as me from the day I was born until the day I was taken into care, and he had witnessed the many, many beatings our mother had given me, without ever once seeing me do anything that might have warranted them.

Michael had told me he didn't want me to go home again, now Ben had severed all contact with me, and as they were the two people I loved most, there really didn't seem to be anything in my life worth living for.

Chapter 11

There wasn't really any aspect of life at Denver House that was easy or made you feel good about yourself. No one seemed to look at anything from our point of view and try to think of ways to make things better and more manageable for us. Even something simple like doing our own washing was fraught with anxiety – although that wasn't really the staff's fault; it was more to do with the fact that kids would sometimes grab random items out of the washing machine and run around waving them over their heads. It was just a silly game, but I was very self-conscious about my laundry, because I would often return from the places Pete took me to with my knickers stained with blood and semen. So rather than putting them in a washing machine, I used to wash them by hand in the sink in my bedroom, which didn't really get them clean. Which was why, one day, when I was going home on a visit, I decided to take some washing with me.

After Michael had told me they didn't want me to go home anymore, my social worker eventually persuaded me to visit my family again, and when I turned up on the doorstep, feeling sick with anxiety, Mum had let me in. I'd been back a few times since then, but I don't know why I thought Mum would simply accept the fact that I'd brought my washing home and let me get on with doing it, particularly as she had never once in my entire life done anything to try to help me. So I shouldn't have been as surprised as I was when I asked her, nervously, if I could use her washing machine and she grabbed the carrier bag I was clutching and pulled out a pair of knickers.

'Mum, no. Please,' I said, trying to snatch them out of her hand. But she punched my arm, turned away to examine them and shouted, 'What the fuck is this?' Then she showed them to Dad, who pinched his nostrils dramatically, and they both laughed.

'You're disgusting,' Mum said, throwing the knickers at me. And there didn't seem to be any point in denying it or telling her yet again that I wasn't sleeping with men because I wanted to.

Most of the time, life at Denver House followed what had become a normal pattern for me. I would get a phone call from Pete, or from one of his friends, telling me where and when I would be picked up, sometimes with Natalie, sometimes not. Then I'd be driven to a gloomy house somewhere, where I'd be given alcohol, cannabis and occasionally amphetamines. It was the drink I always looked forward to, because it helped to empty my mind before I was taken upstairs by the first of the men who were going to have sex with me that night.

Just because I'd accepted it all and tried to blank it out didn't mean I wasn't desperate, and when Frances started to take an interest in me, it couldn't have come at a better time. One evening she told me, 'I've got some questions I want to ask you, Zoe. I'll come up to your room when I'm on shift tonight.' Mostly what she wanted to know about was stuff to do with my mum and the way she'd treated me before I was taken into care, but she also asked me to give her Pete's phone number and the numbers of some of the other men who picked me up.

Because she spoke to me differently from the way most of the other staff members did and seemed to have a genuine interest in me, I really thought she was going to do something to help me. So I couldn't understand why nothing happened as a result of what I told her, particularly because I knew that everything any of the kids at Denver House said or did was supposed to be recorded in their files. It wasn't until recently that I found out she rarely made notes about any of our conversations, even though what I told her confirmed what most of the staff already knew, or at least suspected, before I ever went there – that there was *something* going on. In fact, whenever Frances did make a note of anything I told her, she would preface it by saying she had been doing her normal evening rounds and I'd asked to talk to her. Which wasn't true, because

I only ever spoke to her about any of it when she came to my room and asked me questions. So I don't know why she said that, or why she wanted to know about what had happened if she wasn't going to act on what I said and try to help me.

I'd been told when I first arrived at Denver House that I must *not* have any physical contact with anyone in the unit, neither staff nor other kids. But when Frances was on night shift, she would give me a hug and kiss the top of my head when she said goodnight, and sometimes she'd wake me up to say goodbye and give me another kiss and a hug when she was going off duty. It doesn't sound like much, I know, but it had huge significance for me, because, apart from the quick hug my key worker had given me the day I'd 'rescued' her from being verbally abused by some of the lads, Frances was the first person ever to have hugged me.

'You know more about me than any of the members of staff here,' she used to say. 'I think about you a lot when I'm not at work.' And when she came in on Christmas Day even though she wasn't on shift, she told me, 'I've said I've come to see everyone, but really I've just come in to see you.'

For a child who had only ever been spoken to nicely by teachers, and who, at the age of 14, had only been touched in anger or during unwanted sexual intercourse, the kindness and affection Frances began to show me made me feel very special. So I was confused when she still sometimes bullied me, and I didn't know what I'd done to upset her when she said things to me like, 'I'm the only friend you've got in this place. You'd do well to remember that, Zoe Patterson.' In fact, another member of staff called Coleen overheard her on that occasion and came up to my room a bit later to ask if I was all right – and then, when I said I was, to tell me all about her aches and pains and about how glad she was to be nearing retirement age!

It's exhausting and very soul-destroying thinking that you're always in the wrong. I seemed to have spent my entire life being punished for something by my mum, or punishing myself because I believed I was useless and that everything bad was my fault. So I took the blame without questioning it when, not long after Frances started coming to my room in the evenings, I seemed constantly to be writing notes to her telling her how sorry I was for upsetting her, without ever really knowing what I was apologising for.

I'd been at Denver House for several months when one of the lads told me that Frances used to wake him up in the middle of the night and take him to play pool in the pool room. 'She's stopped doing it since she started liking you,' he said, and when I saw how upset he was about it, I felt guilty about that too.

One evening when Frances was on waking night duty, I was lying in my bed, listening to music on my headphones and watching the shadows on the ceiling, when she came bursting into my room and started pacing up and down, saying, 'I can't do this anymore. You're going to get me into trouble.'

'Can't do what?' I asked anxiously. 'What have I done?' But she just threw her hands up in the air dramatically and said again, 'I *just* can't do it,' then walked out of my room, leaving me to wonder what was wrong with me that made me do whatever it was I'd done to upset the one person who was nice to me. Because she was nice to me, some of the time, and I was desperately anxious not to lose her friendship, even though I hated it when she made jokes at my expense, which she often did, or asked me in a mocking voice, 'Ooh, have you got a boyfriend then, Zoe?' Which was particularly embarrassing and hurtful when she knew I was being trafficked and abused on a regular basis.

It wasn't until years later that I realised I didn't do anything to upset Frances, and that perhaps the main reason why I was so distressed and confused by her behaviour towards me was because it was similar to the way my mother had always treated me – although Frances never beat me and my mother never said anything nice to me. What *was* the same, however, was the way I was always trying to work out what I'd done wrong, when the truth was I hadn't done anything at all and it was their own 'issues' that made them want to control and manipulate a little girl who was so obviously anxious to please them so that they'd like, or love, her.

What I also discovered later was that I wasn't the only girl Frances manipulated. In fact, a girl who came to the unit for a while not very long after Abbie left got in touch with me a few years ago and said that while she was living at Denver House, she'd had 'a relationship' with Frances. I knew Frances was married and had three children, and she often used to talk about the problems she was having with one of them. But maybe she was struggling with her own sexuality at the time, and for some reason it made her feel better about herself to use the crush I had on her to make *me* feel worse. Because I knew by that time that I was gay.

I'd actually realised when I was ten, although because I didn't know anything about sex or sexuality at that age, I didn't understand what it meant. I did understand it by the time I went to Denver House, however, and I knew I had to keep it a secret, because everyone in a place like that pretends – to themselves and to everyone else – that they're 'normal' and tough and not to be messed with, and it isn't a good idea to give anyone a reason even to suspect that you might be 'different' in any way. That's why I hated it whenever Frances asked me in front of the other kids if I had a boyfriend, then laughed when I blushed and stared at my feet. Because not only did she know about all the horrible things that were happening to me, I think she also knew I was gay, and was just amusing herself by playing games with me.

Perhaps it's something to do with the human spirit in general, or maybe I was born with some sort of innate optimism that has persisted – sometimes almost imperceptibly – even during periods when I couldn't have dredged up a single memory of a positive experience. Whatever the reason, and despite – or perhaps because of – everything that was happening at Denver House, I always held on to the belief that one day I would meet someone special. That was what I was waiting for and sometimes, when I hit rock bottom like I did after my brother Ben told me not to call him again, it was the only thing that stopped me taking my own life.

You don't think of yourself as a kid when you are one, but when I look back on it now, I realise that we were all just kids trying to get by in whatever way we could. And the one thing we had in common – even the aggressive kids who didn't seem to give a shit what anyone thought about them – was that we were trying to deal with the fact that no one cared about us or expected us to do or achieve anything good.

Things should be different now that it's mandatory for the staff in children's homes to have at least a Level 2 NVQ in Health and Social Care. At that time, however, someone like Des, for example, could go straight from his job as a kitchen fitter to working at Denver House. So perhaps it wasn't surprising that it often felt as though we didn't matter to anyone – after all, not even our own families wanted us – and that the staff were just there to contain us until we were old enough to be dumped back into society and expected to look after ourselves.

There was one night when things kicked off really badly – which happened quite a lot, particularly with the lads –

and a kid ended up having to go to hospital because a window was slammed shut on his finger. One member of staff called Julie, who was a nice woman in her early fifties, was really shaken up about it and I can remember her saying to me, 'I only do this job part-time to earn some money to pay for my fags.'

'Yeah, but *you're* all right,' I told her. 'You actually listen.'

I don't think she said anything more at the time, but when I bumped into her four or five years later she told me, 'I'm glad I've seen you, Zoe. I wanted to say thank you. I was going to quit the job and walk out that night, but what you said made me stay.' So I was glad I'd seen her too, because I couldn't believe that something I'd said had had an effect on someone else's life like that, and it made me feel really good. She was an exception though, and there were several occasions when members of staff aggravated situations that could have been dealt with and contained and made them into something much bigger and scarier than they might otherwise have been.

Most of the teasing and minor incidents of bullying that were part of living somewhere like Denver House didn't really mean anything, and I didn't have any problems with any of the kids there, except for Natalie of course, and she pretty much left me alone as long as I did what I was told. The only thing that really scared me was someone kicking off, because sometimes the kids just seemed to lose control, and then you didn't know what they might do. So I was *very* frightened the night a member of staff overreacted to a very minor incident and ended up triggering what almost amounted to a riot.

I'd had a huge row with Natalie earlier that evening, because I'd finally stood up for myself and refused to go with her to be picked up by Pete. I was just leaving the office when she'd come to find me and she'd had Debbie with her, the girl I'd gone out on a limb for after I'd seen the look of fear on her face when she was picking up clothes from Natalie's bedroom floor. Although I knew Natalie had started taking Debbie out to meet men, we'd never gone at the same time – until now apparently – and I think it was seeing the crushed, defeated expression on Debbie's face that gave me the courage to say I couldn't go.

Unlike some of the other kids in the unit, Natalie's aggression wasn't just bravado, or a front to make her seem tougher than she was really was. I'd met her mum – an intimidating woman with spiky blonde hair and numerous tattoos and body piercings – so I knew she came from a tough family. In fact, on one of the couple of occasions her mum came to visit Natalie at the unit, she said she liked the cap I was wearing and that she wanted it, and it didn't even cross my mind not to whip it off my head immediately and hand it to her.

So it was the first time I had ever stood up to Natalie, and I don't know whether I'd have had the nerve to do it again on any other night, or if I'd have been so brave *that* night if we hadn't been standing near the open door of the office. Natalie obviously didn't care that the members of staff who were in the office at the time had heard her say to me, 'Oh, there you are. I've been looking for you. Come on. It's time to go.' But she must have realised that threatening me when I refused would have been a step too far, because she just shot me a look that said quite clearly, 'Just you wait. You'll pay for this,' then put her hand on Debbie's shoulder and almost shoved her out of the front door.

I liked Debbie. Whenever Natalie wasn't around – which wasn't often, unfortunately – we used to sneak off together to buy some cider, then find a derelict building or some other sheltered and deserted spot where we could sit and drink it. We didn't ever talk about what happened when Natalie took us out with her. We just chatted about stuff that didn't matter and tried to shut out the real world for a couple of hours and feel like normal kids our age must feel. So I felt really bad for her, and guilty about the fact that she was having to go with Natalie after I'd got out of it. I was angry too, because if the members of staff in the office *had* heard what was going on right outside the door, why hadn't they said anything or tried to intervene? Why had they let Natalie take another young girl who had been placed in their care to meet men who would do things to her that would hurt her physically and psychologically, and very probably ruin the rest of her life?

I think the reason I stood up to Natalie that evening was because the suicidal thoughts I'd been having for some time had recently become all-consuming. So if I was going to kill myself anyway, her threats lost a lot of their power. My courage evaporated as soon as I got up to my room, however, and after sitting on my bed for a while, imagining what Natalie would do to me when she got back later that night, I decided to run away.

There was a woman called Kath, who lived with her teenage daughter just a few streets away from Denver House and who used to let us drink at her house – sometimes as a 'reward' when some of the lads shoplifted alcohol for her. That's where I went that evening, and after getting drunk with Kath and her daughter, she let me stay the night.

It wouldn't have been difficult for Natalie to guess where I'd be – she knew I didn't have anywhere else to go – and the next morning she came looking for me. Fortunately, we saw her walking up the front path and ran into the hallway, where Kath opened the cupboard under the stairs, pushed aside some boxes with her foot to create a space just big enough for me crawl into, and said, 'Quick! Hide in here.'

I was so scared I was crying as I sat there, clutching my knees to my chest and biting my lip so that I didn't make any sound as Kath opened the front door.

'She's here, isn't she?' I heard Natalie say.

'No. Who?' Kath asked.

I had to stifle a sob when Natalie answered aggressively, 'Zoe. I know she's here, Kath. There's no point pretending she isn't.'

'No, Zoe isn't here.' Kath's casual indifference sounded convincing. 'I haven't seen her for a few days.'

'Well, if you do,' Natalie said, with slightly less certainty now, 'tell her to watch her back, because when I find her – and I *will* find her – I'm going to beat her up.'

I was shaking as I crawled out of the cupboard and followed Kath and her daughter into the kitchen, where she handed me a can of lager. I stayed with them, drinking, for the rest of the day, but I knew I couldn't hide for ever, and as I had nowhere else to go, I returned to the unit that evening, dreading the prospect of having to face Natalie and very frightened of what she was going to do to me.

Chapter 12

I could hear people shouting and the sound of breaking glass before I'd even turned the corner into the street where the unit was, and by the time I got there all hell was breaking loose.

I found out later that one of the lads had refused to leave the pool room when he was told to, and Des – the member of staff who had spoken to Yvonne after the incident in the kitchen – had exacerbated the situation by dragging him out from under the pool table, giving him some bad carpet burns in the process, and then forcefully restraining him.

I don't know whether the boy had been doing something that justified Des's reaction, but it wouldn't have been the first time a member of staff's response was often out of all proportion to what had happened. Instead of calming things down, they sometimes seemed to exacerbate relatively minor situations, which then ended up with other kids getting angry too. Apparently, that's what had happened that night, only this time it resulted in uproar and the staff locking themselves in the office. It wasn't my fight though, and I was scared. So I crept up to my room, packed some stuff into my school bag, and walked out.

I was just approaching the car park when I saw Natalie. She was with a bunch of lads who were smashing the windows of Des's car, and I was just wondering if I could sneak past without her seeing me when she turned around. My heart was thudding and she was starting to walk towards me when a member of staff put his head out of the office window and shouted, 'The police are on their way.'

'I'll deal with you later,' Natalie said. Then she joined all the other kids who had started running off in every direction, while I walked across the car park and out on to the street.

It was the middle of the night and about a 40-minute walk to my parents' house, but I didn't have anywhere else to go. So I set off in the darkness, frightened of my own shadow whenever I walked under a street light, and tried not to think about where I had just come from or where I was going.

I must have been about halfway home when Frances drove past me. Des, the member of staff whose car windows had just been smashed, was sitting in the passenger seat beside her but didn't see me, and she just raised her hand in acknowledgement, then continued on her way.

After Dad stopped working and Mum started drinking even more than she'd done before, she slept downstairs every night, and because I knew she'd probably still be up and in the kitchen, I walked down the side of the house and knocked on the back door. I don't remember what she said when she opened it and saw me standing there, just that it was something nasty that made me even more anxious because I thought she might not let me in. But she did, and after telling her what had happened, I was asking if I could come back and live at home when Dad came into the kitchen, and before she had a chance to say anything, he said, 'Yeah, you can stay. I'll ring them in the morning and tell them you'll be living here from now on.' So she just shrugged and turned her back on us.

I hadn't ever stayed overnight at my parents' house since I'd left there more than a year ago, and my bedroom was exactly as it had been, except that the bed had been made, using the same, unwashed, sheets. But at least I could go to sleep knowing that Natalie wasn't going to knock on my door and beat me up.

The next morning, Dad walked down to the phone box at the end of the street and told someone at Denver House that I wasn't going back. A couple of days later, horrible Yvonne came to the house to drop off the rest of my stuff and tell me, with spiteful satisfaction, 'You do know that that's it now. You can't change your mind, whatever happens.' I'd been feeling bad enough already, and didn't need to be reminded that I was now trapped at home without any options.

It wasn't until some time later that I even thought to wonder why social services allowed me to go back home after the investigation that had been carried out more than a year earlier had resulted in a decision being made that it was an 'unsafe place' for me to live and that I should remain in care until I was 18. Perhaps I slipped through the net for some reason. Or maybe they thought, as my mum did, that I was a problem they could do without, which is what I suspected when I did realise that they'd done the wrong thing.

I think I was a bit surprised when Mum just seemed to accept that I was back and treated me pretty much the way she'd always done, except that she hit me a bit less often than she used to do before I went away. Unfortunately, she played mind games instead, which in some ways were even more damaging.

She still gave me whisky and cola to take to school every day. My teachers knew I was drinking and sometimes one of them would ask me, 'Have you drunk anything this morning?' And when I said that I had, she'd tell me, 'Well, try not to have any more till dinner time.' I suppose she didn't know what else to say. But it wasn't as easy as that. Even after I went home, I was still being trafficked, mostly to places in and around Birmingham, and however many times I told my parents about what was happening, my father just said horrible things to me like, 'What you need is a big black dick inside you.'

Also, thanks to Mum's carefully orchestrated manipulation, I was even more afraid than before of waking up one night to find Dad standing by my bed, particularly after she told me one day, 'I saw your dad in your bedroom this morning when you were at school. I couldn't work out what he was doing at first. Then I realised he was sniffing your underwear. You should start arranging the things in your drawers so that you'll be able to tell if he's been touching them.' And when I went up to my room to check as soon as I got home from school the next day, I found that she was right and things *had* been moved.

Although I didn't realise it at the time, Mum was using my fear of Dad to manipulate me, and after she'd done everything she could think of to make me afraid to go to sleep at night, she started saying things like, 'You could just push him down the stairs when he's drunk. It would be like an accident.' I think now that it was all part of some distorted plan she had to get rid of him, and potentially me too, because she could then have said I'd done it deliberately because I was afraid of him sexually abusing me. But although I *was* afraid of him, he was still my dad, and I had no desire at all to see him dead, any more than I wished the same fate for my mum, who really *had* been abusing me, physically and mentally, for as long as I could remember.

The reality of living at home again was even more horrible than I'd expected it to be. In fact, the only positive aspect – or at least it seemed positive to me at the time – was that Mum bought whisky for me. Self-harming helped a bit too, and when Mum found out what I was doing, she took a knife out of the drawer in the kitchen, sharpened it, then thrust it into my hand saying, 'If you're going to do it, why not do a proper job?'

I knew what she was saying, that rather than just making cuts on my arms and legs I should kill myself. It was something I thought about almost constantly anyway. But when I took the knife up to my room, I just ran its razor-sharp blade across the skin of my legs and arms, while Mum stayed downstairs in the kitchen, probably hoping I was doing something 'right' at last.

Mum had always blamed her drinking on me, and now Dad did too, saying that I was the reason she was the way she was. And although I felt resentful about the fact that everyone blamed me for their problems, I had been told so often, for as long as I could remember, that everything bad was my fault there was a part of me that believed it was true and I felt guilty because of it.

Looking back on it all now, it looks like a huge mess.

I had meetings with my social worker from time to time, but nothing was ever done about anything I told her. So I continued to get texts and phone calls from Pete, sometimes during the day, but more often in the early evening. And because I was afraid of him, and of Natalie, I would leave the house and go to wherever he told me to meet him.

My parents didn't pay me any attention at all, except when they needed a scapegoat or a target for their spiteful jokes, so they didn't ever ask me where I was going, or care if I was in or out. I found out later that when I was living at Denver House a member of staff used to phone my parents whenever I went missing, until Mum told them one day to stop bothering her every time it happened, 'Because she's not our problem anymore. She's yours.'

I was still trying to do my best at school, but I found it increasingly difficult to focus. And when I wasn't at school or being trafficked by Pete and his friends, I stayed in my room. I did occasionally go out with friends from school though, and it was on one of those nights out, after I'd been living at home for about six months, that I lost the mobile phone Pete had given me.

My first reaction when I couldn't find it was total panic and I started frantically searching for it, checking and rechecking every pocket in my jacket while repeating over and over in my head, 'It must be here. It must be.' But it wasn't. So then I sat on the floor in my bedroom, crying and trying not to imagine what Pete – or Natalie – would do the next time he phoned me and I didn't pick up. But the more I thought about it, the more I began to wonder what they *could* do, because I always met them some distance from my house and they didn't know where I lived. So if they couldn't contact me by phone …

My heart was racing as I considered the possibilities: (1) that I might bump into Pete or Natalie in town somewhere; and (2) that Natalie might come looking for me at my school. The first seemed unlikely, as Pete had a Birmingham accent and obviously knew his way around the city far better than he did around the town where I lived, which had always made me think he actually lived in Birmingham rather than locally; and, in any case, I very rarely went into town. As for the second possibility, I knew Natalie wasn't from the area either and she didn't know where I went to school.

Neither argument was foolproof, however, and I spent the next few days anxiously looking over my shoulder all the time when I was out, until eventually I began to think that maybe it really was all over. After almost two years of living in constant fear, being bullied and abused, all it took to put an end to it was to get rid of the phone. Why hadn't I thought of it before? More to the point, why hadn't my key worker or my social worker or any of the other people who used to attend all those pointless meetings about my 'care plan' thought of it? When I told them Pete had given me a mobile phone, why didn't they take it, then move me away from Denver House to somewhere I might have been safe?

When I'd shown the social worker and the woman from the NSPCC the bruises on my legs more than 18 months ago and told them they'd been caused by my mum beating me, I did it because I was desperate to get away from home and because I thought I'd be put in a foster home. Instead, I was put in Denver House – 'Just for six weeks,' they'd said, 'while we do an assessment.' But I'd ended up staying there for a year, because, as I found out later, they had assessed Mum and Dad too and decided they were not 'fit parents'.

They had to put me somewhere, I suppose, once they realised what was happening at home, and I can understand that emergency accommodation might have been difficult to find. What I still don't understand, however, is why they allowed me to stay in Denver House for all those months, when, apparently, it was already 'known to be targeted for prostitution'. I was shocked when I discovered they already knew that. They shouldn't have put anyone in that place, but especially not a vulnerable teenage girl. And I was angry too, because all the time that I was suffering horrific sexual abuse, thinking it must be my fault and unable to understand why no one did anything to help me when I told them what was happening, they *knew* I was telling the truth and that I wasn't doing it because I wanted to, which is what they told my parents.

I kept begging my social worker and the staff at the unit to do *something* to make it stop. But they just let me struggle on, trying to cope with having things done to me that should never be done to anyone of any age, things that were going to affect me for the rest of my life, and that could have resulted in me being killed, or killing myself. Then I lost the phone and it stopped. It makes me incredibly sad to think that it could all have been so easily prevented.

It's a terrible, destructive, life-changing experience to be sexually abused. For me – and I'm sure for many other children in similar situations – it's also incredibly damaging to know that your own parents don't like or care about you. And during those months after I left Denver House and went back to live at home, my mum made it even more clear to me than she'd done before that I was not loved by anyone in my family and no one wanted me around.

It was only quite recently that I began to understand why I've done some of the things I've done and why it can be so difficult for people to change patterns of behaviour that have become established over a period of years, especially, perhaps, during childhood. For me, one of those patterns of behaviour – which is certainly the most destructive – has been drinking. I know my teachers were worried about me and that they often reported their concerns to social services, but no one seemed to take them seriously.

One Friday afternoon, after I'd been living at home for almost 18 months, I waited until all the other kids had left the classroom at the end of the last lesson and told my teacher I couldn't face another weekend of abuse at home.

'I'm so sorry, Zoe,' she said. 'I'd like to be able to offer you more than sympathy, but I'm afraid there isn't much we can do.'

I suppose I hadn't really expected her to say anything very different. But I'd finally reached the point of no return, and instead of walking out of the classroom and going home, I pulled a small kitchen knife out of my school bag and told my teacher, 'I *can't* spend another weekend at home. I'm going to kill myself.'

Although I'd been drinking since first thing in the morning, it wasn't just the alcohol talking. I really couldn't take any more of my father's horrible comments, my mum's violence and nasty remarks, and my parents' constant, vicious arguments and fights. So it was a desperate cry for help, and although I didn't *want* to kill myself, I couldn't see any other way out.

My teacher took a step backwards when I pulled the knife out of my bag, then raised her hand in an instinctively protective gesture as she said, 'It's all right, Zoe. Just wait here while I go and find out what we can do to help you. Don't do anything, will you? Promise me. I'll only be *two* minutes.' And I probably *had* only been sitting there crying for a couple of minutes when she came back with another teacher and told me, 'We've called the police and they're on their way. We had to do it, Zoe. We're very concerned about you.'

By the time the police arrived, I was sitting with the two teachers in an office near the school's reception area, a bit calmer than I had been, but still holding the knife, which I handed to a police officer when he asked me to. No one tried to restrain me or handcuff me on that occasion though. In fact, it was the first time a police officer had ever been nice to me and treated me sympathetically.

I didn't say much to the child protection officer who interviewed me at the police station, just that it wasn't safe for me to go home. Then I was taken by a couple of different policemen to a hospital I didn't know, where I was met by a social worker I'd never seen before, who said they were going to do a mental health assessment so that a decision could be made about where to place me.

The social worker waited outside the room while the psychiatrist asked me questions, which included things like, 'Do you ever hear voices?' and 'Do you know what day it is today?'

'No, I don't ever hear voices,' I said. Then I told him the day and the date, before adding, 'I'm not crazy. I'm just desperately unhappy living at home.' And eventually, after he'd asked me some more questions and I'd shown him the bruises that almost covered my upper arms and the backs of my legs, he said I didn't need to be an inpatient in the hospital and that the solution to my depression would be for me to be removed from the situation that was causing it. Then it was my turn to wait outside while he spoke to the social worker, who eventually drove me to a foster home.

Chapter 13

I didn't ever see that social worker again, but the impression she made on me as she drove me to the foster home has stayed with me – for reasons that weren't entirely good! After telling me she only worked at weekends and only ever on the emergency team, 'Because the pay's much better and we don't always get called out,' she said her manager had hoped I'd be sectioned because she'd been having trouble trying to find a bed for me. 'So this foster home is only a temporary, emergency measure,' she said. Then she sang an old Isley Brothers' song called 'Harvest for the World', and continued to sing for the rest of the journey. Maybe she thought she was cheering me up, but it did make me wonder for a moment if I *had* lost the plot, because she seemed to be in a world of her own, and completely oblivious to my distress.

It was late when I arrived at the foster home that night, and after I'd met my foster carer Sandra and her husband

Bill, I went straight to bed. So I didn't see any of the other kids who were living there until the next morning. It was Saturday, and after Sandra had sorted out the other children, she took me home to pick up my uniform, school bag and a couple of other items of clothing, which was more or less everything I possessed.

My parents still didn't have a phone in the house, so I think someone from social services must have gone round the previous evening to tell them I wasn't coming back. Dad wasn't there when we arrived, and Mum didn't really say anything much, perhaps because she felt a bit intimidated by Sandra, who was a big, no-nonsense sort of woman who could be quite scary when she was angry and who gave the very distinct impression that she would be perfectly capable of looking after herself in almost any situation.

However badly children are treated by their parents, there seems to be a part of them that always longs to be loved by their mum and dad. And although that was true of me for many years, by the time I went home to pick up my things with Sandra that day, I just wanted to get away from them. I'd gone home the night everything kicked off at Denver House because I had nowhere else to go and I'd told myself, 'Maybe things will be different this time.' But I hadn't expected to stay there for more than a few days, and I didn't want to be there that day with Sandra either. So I just grabbed my stuff and got out as quickly as I could.

Sandra and Bill lived in a large house that was actually two semi-detached houses knocked together, with most of the rooms divided with plasterboard, which made it seem more like a children's home than the family home I used to imagine living in one day with foster parents who were just like my friend Carly's mum and dad. But at least it wasn't *my* family home, or Denver House.

There were already *12* kids living in the foster home, although I didn't see many of them on that first day. Some of them were being fostered long term, some just stayed for a few days or weeks before others came to take their place, and one younger and two older ones had actually been adopted by Sandra and Bill. Twelve kids is a lot to have living in any one household. Twelve kids with issues can make even a large house feel crowded and chaotic, and there seemed to be children everywhere. I was one of the lucky ones, however, because I had a small room to myself, which was on the second floor and actually half of what had originally been a not very large bedroom.

It was only Sandra who was the foster carer. Bill – a skinny, bald, very quiet man who looked even smaller than he actually was beside his much bigger wife – had a full-time job and was hardly ever at home and when he was, he didn't really engage with any of the children, not even the ones they'd adopted. Which meant that Sandra had almost sole responsibility for the care of 12 kids with emotional and/or behavioural problems. So perhaps it wasn't surprising that she didn't have the time – or, apparently, the inclination – to offer any of us emotional support and make it seem less like a hostel and more like a home.

Even though I was 15½ when I was fostered, and much less naive than I'd been when I went to live at Denver House, it was still a bit daunting to go, literally overnight, from sitting alone in my bedroom at home to living in a house full of noisy kids again. But I knew I couldn't cope with being at home anymore and that I was just going to have to resign myself to whatever happened next.

I didn't have much contact with the other kids in the house and when I did have a brief chat with an older boy after I'd been there for a few days and mentioned that I thought Sandra was okay, he laughed and said, 'That's because you're still in the two-week honeymoon period. You wait. You'll meet the real Sandra soon.' And he was right. After I'd been there for almost exactly two weeks, Sandra told me, 'There are rules in this house. One of them is that after 8 o'clock in the evening, you do not come downstairs or bother me or Bill for any reason.'

I was used to spending time in my room at home, so I knew I wouldn't have any problem doing it again now. It was just that the way she said it made me feel sad and alone again, and finally shattered the dream I'd always had of living with foster parents who cared about me, maybe even liked me.

Over the next few days, it became increasingly apparent that Sandra saw her only job as being to provide food and accommodation for as many kids as social services were prepared to let her cram into the house. Apart from making a roast dinner on Sundays, she didn't do any cooking for us older kids. 'You make your own meals and do your own washing up,' she told me the day the 'honeymoon period' ended. 'This isn't a hotel, so don't expect people to do it for you.' She opened the door of the fridge as she spoke, pointed to the own-brand food from a cheap local supermarket on the lower shelves and said, 'That's yours.' Then she indicated some items in 'Tesco finest' packaging on the top shelf and added, 'And *that* is for Bill and me *only*. It is *not* to be touched by anyone else.'

I never did do any cooking for myself though. I didn't know how to – Mum had always brought a plate of oven-cooked food up to my room when I was at home, and a chef made all our meals at Denver House – and I didn't have enough confidence to ask Sandra to teach me. I wouldn't have wanted to eat in the kitchen anyway, because I still had huge problems with food. In fact, just the thought of having to sit down with a knife and fork and eat in front of other people made me feel sick with anxiety. So I would go to the corner shop to buy sandwiches and crisps, then eat them alone in my room, just like I used to do when I lived with my parents.

Something else I was anxious about when I lived in the foster home was the fact that Denver House was just a five-minute walk away and I had to pass it on my way to catch the bus to and from school every day. I always walked on the other side of the road with my head down and my fists clenched, but just knowing it was there made me feel as though I hadn't really got away from it at all, not least because it was obvious that what had happened to me was still happening to other girls who lived there, who I sometimes saw getting into cars that pulled up right outside the building.

I didn't recognise any of the men I saw hanging around there. Apart from Pete and a couple of his friends who used to pick me up regularly, I wouldn't have been able to identify any of the other men who abused me, because I always tried not to look at their faces. I doubt whether any of them would have recognised me either, although there was one taxi driver who followed me down the road one day when I was walking back from school and told me to get into his taxi, so maybe he'd seen me before. Fortunately though, I was close to a side road and when he kept insisting and wouldn't leave me alone, I was able to run down an alleyway where he couldn't follow me in his car.

On another day when I was on the way back from school and not far from Denver House, I saw Frances. I was standing talking to a girl called Paula, who I'd just bumped into, after having last seen her when we were both about seven years old and she left the primary school we went to. We'd recognised each other immediately as we were passing, and she was just telling me that she'd recently gone to live at Denver House when Frances appeared and asked me to go round the corner with her because there was something she wanted to talk to me about.

It felt a bit awkward, leaving Paula standing there, but I went, and as soon as we were out of earshot, Frances explained that the reason she'd suggested it was 'because Paula would get jealous'. I didn't know what she meant and was just about to ask her, 'Jealous of what?' when a gust of wind caught the hem of the top she was wearing and folded it up, exposing her stomach and the lower part of her chest. I thought she'd be as embarrassed as I was, so I looked away, but instead of covering herself up, she just laughed and said, 'Ooh, look Zoe, the wind is blowing my skirt up.'

'It's not your skirt. It's your top,' I told her, the awkwardness of the moment making me terse. And after she'd pulled it down again, she asked me for the address and phone number of the foster home where I was living.

A couple of weeks later, she came to the house and was really nice to me, picking me up in her car and taking me to the shopping centre in town, where she told me, 'I want to buy you something, Zoe.' But although we looked round all the clothes shops, I didn't see anything I wanted. So the next time she came she took me to McDonald's and bought Happy Meals for both of us, and when we discovered that we had the same Care Bears, she said, 'Yours is called Flora and mine is Smiley. I'm going to keep Smiley next to the rear-view mirror in my car so that she'll remind me of you when I see her every day.' I can remembering thinking how nice it was to have someone in my life who seemed to care about me, even though I found some of the things she said confusing and got the impression that she wasn't very happy herself.

A few weeks later, I went to Denver House to see Paula and we went out together for the evening. After persuading someone to take our money and buy us a small bottle of vodka in a local shop, we sat on a bench overlooking the graves behind a church, just talking and drinking. I'd had a feeling after I'd spoken to her when we bumped into each other on the street that Paula might be gay, and when I told her I was – which was the first time I'd ever admitted it to anybody – we shared a kiss.

When I saw Frances a few days later, she told me there had been a photograph of me in the office at Denver House, which Paula had stolen and put in her room. 'I know you left the unit together the other evening,' Frances said. 'What did you two get up to?' So I told her about the vodka and sitting in the churchyard, but not about the kiss, although I did wonder if Paula had mentioned it.

Even when I was living in the foster home, I didn't know what it was like to feel safe. At home, I'd always been afraid of my parents. At Denver House, I'd been frightened of Abbie and then, even more so, of Natalie. Now, at the age of 15, I was scared of a boy called Harry.

Harry was one of the two older boys Sandra and Bill had adopted, and he was a bully. Sandra used to buy cigarettes for me, and I was sitting reading on my bed one day when Harry burst into my room without knocking and said, 'Give us some fags.' I almost jumped out of my skin when he barged in, but although I was always frightened of any kind of confrontation, I knew that if I didn't at least try to stand up to him, he would see me as an easy target and then I'd never be free of his bullying. So I said 'No', and I continued to refuse until he hit me, then kept on hitting me until I took half the cigarettes out of the packet and threw them on the bed.

I'd been right to think he'd consider me an easy target, because he did the same thing several times a week after that, and when I threatened to tell Sandra, he just laughed and said, 'Go on. I dare you. She won't believe you. Then you'll have to move out and go and live in one of those residential homes for kids that not even the worst foster parents are prepared to put up with.'

Compared to Harry, I thought Keith, the other older boy Sandra and Bill had adopted, was quite nice, until a younger girl called Rachel, who they fostered at around the same time as me, told me he was sneaking into her room at night and sexually abusing her. I don't think it even crossed my mind to tell anyone what Rachel said. I just assumed that sexual abuse was normal for 'girls like us', and I knew from my own experience that nobody would do anything about it. So instead of asking anyone for help, Rachel and I decided that we would run away together the following day.

The problem was, we couldn't think of anywhere to go and ended up just walking around all day before going back to the foster home. It was a school day and Sandra shouted at us because someone from school had phoned to tell her I'd missed a mock GCSE exam. Then she demanded the bus and dinner money she'd given us that morning, and when we told her we'd spent it – on cider – she got even more angry. I can understand why she was annoyed, but she didn't once ask if we were okay or if there had been some reason why we'd played truant. I don't suppose she cared; she didn't really mind what any of us did as long as we didn't upset the status quo.

I didn't ever let on to anyone about what Rachel had told me. So although I was more wary of Keith after that, he was always okay with me – while we were living under the same roof, at least.

I had been hooked on alcohol before I left Denver House, and during the months when I'd lived at home it was, quite literally, the one thing my mum seemed happy to provide for me. So by the time I went to live in the foster home, I was dependent on it. Sandra had been told about my drink problem before she agreed to foster me, and to begin with she used to think it was funny when I came back from school a bit drunk. Eventually though, when she stopped finding it amusing, she would tell me, 'I don't care what you do as long as you don't cause any trouble. So if you're going to drink, do it upstairs in your room.' Which is where I self-harmed too, when I was feeling really bad.

I'm sure a lot of people would be shocked to think that a teenager could be dependent on alcohol. But if drinking is the only way you can get through the day and you know that if you don't have a drink, you won't be able to push all the horrible things in your life just far enough into the background for you not to kill yourself – on that day, at least – why wouldn't you do it? That's how I felt when I used to hang around outside a local shop, clutching my pocket money, school dinner money and the money for my bus fares that Sandra gave me every day, asking people to buy me a bottle of whisky or some cans of strong lager. Usually, I'd keep back just enough to buy some sandwiches and crisps, but I was quite thin as a teenager and didn't have a big appetite, so I didn't need to set aside much for food.

Sometimes, I'd take the drink back to my room at the foster home, and sometimes I'd tell Sandra I was going out with friends, then find somewhere quiet and out of the way to drink it. The truth was, I didn't really have any friends by that time; I just didn't seem to be able to fit in. And it's hard to keep friendships alive when you're focusing all your attention on trying to survive, which is what I thought I was doing, although, ironically, I was actually putting myself at huge risk on an almost daily basis by asking total strangers to buy drink for me.

There was one evening when I drank the bottle of cider someone had got for me and then decided that I wanted another. I hadn't been standing outside the shop for more than a few seconds when a man who had just pulled up in his car agreed to go in and buy it for me, and when he came out, he asked if I'd like to go for a drive with him. I'd like to think that I'd normally have had more sense than to say yes, but I was already drunk and had had a really bad day.

We'd been driving around for a while, neither of us saying very much, and I'd drunk quite a lot from my second bottle of cider, when the man stopped outside a small terraced house and said, 'This is where I live. I just need to pick something up. Why don't you come in and wait for me?'

One of the main reasons I drank was because it made me feel as though I'd been anaesthetised and was watching everything that was going on around me through a curtain of fog. What it also did, however, was cloud my judgement and suppress my instinct for self-preservation. Which is why I followed the man through the front door and into a room where there was an unmade bed in one corner, a chest of drawers with a lamp on it, and an almost overpowering smell of damp.

I'd been taken to a lot of almost identical houses during the time when I was being trafficked, and the familiarity of the room made me feel instantly anxious. So I was relieved when he left me there and went in search of whatever it was he'd called in for. I sat down on the edge of the unmade bed while I was waiting for him, and I was just standing up as he came back into the room a few minutes later when he pushed me down again, held my head in his hands and tried to kiss me.

I was already feeling queasy because of all the cider I'd drunk, and when I pushed him away and said 'No' very loudly, he punched me in the face. The room seemed to be spinning around me as I lashed out, trying to fight him off as he pulled down my trousers and underwear and raped me.

I was still trying to find the place in my head that would blank it all out so that I could disengage my mind from my body when he squeezed my chest and bit me. It was the shock of him biting me that finally seemed to give me the surge of strength I needed to shove him off me and roll on to the floor, and as I started to crawl away from him, he raped me anally from behind, while I crouched there, sobbing and praying for him to finish.

I didn't know the part of town he'd taken me to, so although I was desperate to get away from him, I accepted his almost casual offer of a lift back to the shop where he'd picked me up, then I walked from there to the foster home. It was November and a very cold night, but although I knocked on the doors and windows for at least half an hour, no one came to let me in. So I curled up on the back doorstep and thought about how much I hated myself and all the men who had ever raped and abused me, until I eventually fell asleep.

In the morning, when Sandra unlocked the back door and let me in, she was really angry with me and demanded to know where I'd been. I'd have been angry with her, too, if I'd been able to feel anything, because I knew she must have heard me knocking in the night and have realised that, by not letting me into the house, she was actually exacerbating the danger I'd already put myself in. But all I wanted by that time was a shower, so I walked past her into the house and up the stairs without speaking to her at all.

I was in the bathroom starting to take off my clothes when I saw the blood on the back of my coat. Apparently Sandra had seen it too, because by the time I'd scrubbed every trace of the man off my bruised body, she had phoned the police and they'd arrived at the house.

I didn't want to talk to anyone; I just wanted to go to bed and sleep. But there didn't seem to be any point in refusing, so I told them what had happened. Then they took the clothes I'd been wearing – unfortunately, I'd already washed away all the evidence from my body – and I agreed to go for an examination and to have photographs taken of my black eye, the bruises on my thighs and arms, and the bite marks on my chest.

Because there were nights when I drank so much I was completely out of it and unable to remember anything that had happened – like the night Sandra said she found me passed out in an alleyway near the house – I had started carrying a piece of paper with me all the time that had Sandra's phone number on it. The man who raped me that night must have found it in my coat pocket, because although he always hid his own number and refused to say who he was, I knew he was the man who kept phoning the house and asking for me. Then, one day, I saw him driving slowly past and managed to get the registration number of his car, which I gave to Sandra and she gave it to the police.

Although the registration number turned out to be false, or to belong to someone else's car, the police did find him, and when he proved to be a match for the DNA that had been found on my coat, he was put on remand. The thought of having to give evidence against him in court was really scary, even if we wouldn't have to come face to face. But it seemed almost like a vindication too, because finally someone would be saying that what had been done to me was wrong. Then, a few months later, the charges against him were dropped when it was decided that, because of my drinking and risk-taking lifestyle, I wouldn't make a reliable witness. They were right, I suppose, although at the time it just seemed to be further proof of the fact that it didn't really matter – that *I* didn't really matter.

Maybe the man eventually got convicted of something though, because I discovered recently that the house he took me to that night was linked to a major investigation the police were already conducting into child sexual exploitation.

During the time I was being fostered, I sometimes went home to see my parents, on visits that always involved Dad saying lewd things that made me feel uncomfortable and often ended with me falling out with my mum. I only went because I felt guilty for having left Mum on her own with him, because although my younger brother was living at home, I don't think he knew about the way Dad sometimes forced himself on her.

The real problem for me, however, was that I always came away from those visits feeling even less self-confident and more miserable than I'd done when I arrived. And it was when I was on my way back to the foster home one day that I had sex with a man in exchange for money for the first time in my life.

Chapter 14

It was early evening and I was standing at a bus stop when a van that had already driven slowly past me a couple of times stopped on the other side of the road and a guy got out of the passenger side. It was only when I realised that he was waving at me that I recognised him as someone I went to school with. So I waved back, then watched him walk off down the road and around the corner.

I must have been standing at the bus stop for almost an hour by that time, and I was just pushing my hands deeper into my pockets and thinking how cold I was when the driver of the van rolled down his window and called across the road to me, 'I think you've missed the last bus.'

'No, there should be another one,' I told him. 'It must have been delayed.'

'Don't forget it's a Bank Holiday,' the man said. 'There's a different timetable.'

My heart sank as I realised he was right and that if I'd set off on foot an hour ago, I'd already be back in my room at the foster home, having the drink I so badly needed.

'I can give you a lift if you like.' He shrugged his shoulders as if to indicate that it was no big deal either way.

My immediate instinct was to say, 'No thanks.' But it was cold and dark, and I knew that if I set off walking now, I wouldn't get back to the house until after the 8 p.m. curfew set by Sandra. And although I didn't know the van driver, he was obviously a friend of someone I *did* know and I wasn't afraid of him. So I accepted his offer of a lift, then crossed the road and climbed up into the seat beside him.

'Are you okay?' he asked as I was doing up my seat belt. 'You looked a bit sad and worried standing there all on your own, waiting for a bus that was never going to come.'

'I've had a row with my parents.' The words tumbled out before I realised I was going to say them.

'So are you running away?'

'No. I was just visiting them. I've lived in a foster home for the last few weeks. Everyone keeps telling me I need to go home from time to time to see my parents so that I don't lose touch with them. The trouble is, every time I do go, it ends badly. Which isn't really surprising, I suppose, when it's *because* of the problems I have with my parents that I'm in a foster home in the first place!'

It was way more information than I'd intended to give him, and more than I would normally have told anyone about myself. But I was upset, and once I started talking about it, I didn't seem to be able to stop, perhaps partly because I was trying to get things clear in my own mind.

'I'm sorry you're in a bad situation,' the man said. 'At least if I give you a lift back to the foster home it will solve your immediate problem and you'll have one thing less to worry about.'

'Thanks,' I muttered, as he did a U-turn in the empty street, then set off in the opposite direction from the way he'd come.

Neither of us spoke again for a few minutes, but when I glanced at him he seemed to be looking at me appraisingly, as if he was trying to decide whether or not to say something to me.

'I'm doing you a big favour,' he said at last, catching my eye.

'Yeah. Thanks. I appreciate it.' I turned to look out of the window beside me.

'A *really* big favour,' he continued. 'So maybe you should do me a favour in return.'

I could feel the permanent knot of anxiety in my stomach tighten, and as I shifted uncomfortably in my seat, trying to think of something to say in response, he added, 'I'll give you 20 quid if you'll have sex with me.'

My immediate reaction was anger, which quickly gave way to hurt, because although what he was suggesting – about the sex, if not about the money – was what I'd learned to expect from men I didn't know, I felt as though

I *did* know him. So I was shocked and upset to realise that he saw me just like all those other men did.

The saddest thing of all, perhaps, was that I was so convinced I was worthless I didn't really think I could say no. So I accepted the man's £20 and stuffed it into the pocket of my jeans. Then he drove to an area of town that was notorious for being frequented by prostitutes and perverts, where I lay on the cold, hard floor at the back of his van while he grunted and stared off into the distance above my head as he penetrated me roughly.

'So that's it,' I thought, as the familiar disembodied feeling descended over me like a cloak of invisibility. 'This is all I'm good for. All those scores of men who hurt and abused me have made me into what they thought I was – a disgusting, filthy, worthless excuse for a human being. Everyone must be able to see that's what I am. I just didn't see it myself. Until now.'

As soon as he'd finished, he zipped up his trousers without saying a word, then got back into the driver's seat and started the engine. I only just had time to pull on my underwear and was still fumbling with the button on my jeans when he accelerated away from the kerb so abruptly I banged my head on the side of the van. Suddenly, I was frightened and my heart was pounding as I reached for the headrest on the passenger seat and pulled myself up so that I could look out of the window.

I could have screamed and banged on the side of the van hoping someone would hear me and phone the police. Or

I could have said something to him. Instead, I stayed silent and tried to memorise the route he was taking, just in case I was wrong and I wasn't about to die. Then, after a few minutes, the panic subsided as abruptly as it had come and I realised I didn't care. Turning away from the windows, I crawled across the metal floor at the back of the van and sat in the middle of it with my legs crossed, like I used to do in my bedroom when I was a little girl so that I would be able to see the monsters – real or imagined – when they opened the door.

I was still scared, but I felt a strange sense of relief too, because if I *was* going to be killed by a stranger, the eternal decision about whether to end my own life or continue my miserable, pointless struggle to survive would have been made for me. My only real concern was that he would do it quickly and painlessly. But even though I welcomed the thought of death and had already decided that I wouldn't struggle or try to fight him off, something inside me seemed to tighten when the van came to an abrupt halt.

There was a sound of metal scraping on metal as the rear door opened and he reached in to grab my arm and pull me out. But instead of dragging me into some dark alleyway or abandoned building plot, he slammed the door shut, jumped back into the driver's seat and drove away, leaving me standing at the side of the road, bemused and disorientated.

It was a few seconds before I realised I was in a street I knew, not far from the foster home. I didn't have any idea what time it was, but maybe, if I hurried, I could get back before 8 p.m. Then I could have a drink from the bottle of whisky I always kept hidden in my room, and no one would ever need to know what I'd done.

Surprisingly perhaps, despite the drinking and the risk-taking, I did sometimes still go to school and try to focus on studying for my GCSE exams. Even during the period when I'd been living at home, I'd been doing quite well at school and it had been predicted that I would get ten GCSEs and eventually go to university. Since I'd been at the foster home, however, my schoolwork had deteriorated.

My teachers seemed to have become resigned to the fact of my drinking and to have decided that as they couldn't do anything to change the situation, they might as well try to ignore it. One of them even helped me to walk across the playground one morning when she saw me drunk and staggering as I tried to get to my next lesson.

In the end, I left school with seven GCSEs, six at grade C and just one grade B, which wasn't bad, I suppose, in view of everything that was going on, but was a huge disappointment to me. The only thing I got any pleasure from during those years was studying and learning new things, and it turned out when the results came in that I wasn't even any good at doing that. Or, at least, that's how it felt.

I was still living in the foster home when I did my GCSEs and after I left school that summer, I went to college to study for A levels in English, Sociology and Psychology. They were subjects that really interested me and I wanted to work hard and do well. Unfortunately, however, I wasn't emotionally mature enough to handle the increased independence of college coupled with the responsibility of having to guide my own studies, and it wasn't long before I started skipping classes.

I'd often use the money Sandra gave me for lunch every morning to buy cider, strong lager or whisky. Then I'd just wander around the streets or go and sit in the children's playground my dad had once taken me to, where the swings and slides were now rusty and broken. The playground was behind a church next to open fields, and I liked it because of that memory and because no one ever seemed to go there except me and a friendly black cat, who always rubbed his head against my legs and purred when I stroked him.

I would sit there for hours, drinking and writing short stories or just listening to music and thinking about my life. Then I'd go back to the foster home and run upstairs before anyone could question me, which was easy to do in a madhouse full of kids. Eventually though, someone from the college started phoning Sandra every time I didn't go in, then she started lying in wait for me and asking sarcastically, 'So, Zoe, did you have a nice day at college today?' Just to let me know she knew.

I was still self-harming, cutting my legs as well as my arms by that time, and one night I made a cut in my wrist that was so deep I couldn't stop it bleeding and had to tell her. I did go into college the next day, and when I came back in the early afternoon and went into the kitchen to get a glass of water, Sandra was there with one of her friends.

I had only just walked through the door when Sandra said, 'Show Fran what you did to yourself last night. Go on, Zoe, show her.' I was really embarrassed and shook my head without saying anything. But she kept insisting, until eventually I pulled up my sleeve, peeled back the bandage, and revealed the red scabbing wound on my wrist to Sandra's friend. Then I fainted.

I think it was the stress of being forced to reveal something about myself I didn't want anyone to know that made me pass out. I'd never done it before, and I can remember feeling scared when everything suddenly seemed to go blurry, then saying to my mum in my head, 'I'm going to have to go now. Someone's talking to me,' and thinking I was being rude because I couldn't answer them.

The next thing I remember is hearing Sandra's friend asking anxiously, 'Is she all right? Should you phone for an ambulance?'

'No. She's fine now,' Sandra answered. 'But you see what I have to put up with! Come on, let's go into town.' It was what they did most days when the younger kids were at school and everyone was out, and Sandra clearly wasn't going to allow a fainting, self-harming teenager to disrupt their plans. So I went upstairs to my room, and a few minutes later heard the front door close behind them.

It was a few weeks after that incident, when I'd been living in the foster home for almost a year, that the placement broke down. For some reason, I'd decided to tell Sandra I was gay, and although I was very anxious about confiding in her, I hadn't expected her to respond the way she did, saying she couldn't cope with me anymore. So it was a planned move. In fact, I discovered recently that she told social services, 'I want her gone by Christmas,' which I didn't know at the time and which I found surprisingly upsetting. I'd always thought that it was my fault the placement broke down, although I realise now that Sandra didn't ever give me the care and emotional support I so desperately needed, and that she did the wrong thing by allowing me to drink.

I did try to engage with the counselling that was organised for me while I was living in the foster home, but I found it really tough. What no one seemed to take into account was that whereas it might make perfect sense to tell a 16-year-old girl who has been repeatedly sexually abused and has a major alcohol problem that she needs to stop drinking, you have to be able to give her a reason for making the huge effort involved in trying to face life sober. And you have to be able to give her the answers to questions like: What is there to look forward to? What will be there to soften the edges of life if I do stop drinking? What does the future hold for me? Because the answers to all those questions was so obviously 'Nothing', the counselling just seemed pointless.

Once it was decided that I was going to have to move on from the foster home, and because I was 16, I was appointed a leaving care worker, who turned out to be Yvonne, the not-always-very-Christian lady from Denver House, who, with some other members of staff, had recently left the unit and joined social services' leaving care team. I was horrified when I found out, and when I told Sandra that I didn't get on with Yvonne and didn't want her to be involved with my case, she said, 'That's fine. I'll sort it out with her when she arrives.'

When the day came, Sandra was as good as her word and told Yvonne pretty much straightaway that I would prefer to have a different leaving care worker.

'Really? Why?' Yvonne's mouth contorted into a tight-lipped smile as she looked at me and asked the question. Unnerved by the cold look in her eyes, I glanced quickly at Sandra, who answered for me.

'It's nothing personal,' she told Yvonne, in a tone of voice that made it clear she wasn't someone who could be bullied and intimidated. 'It's just that she'd prefer it not to be anyone from Denver House.'

'Oh, come along now.' Yvonne's smile got tighter as she turned her attention back to me. 'That's all behind us. It's in the past. We've both started a new chapter in our lives and I'd really like to work with you.'

'I'm sorry,' I said, Sandra's involvement giving me a resolve I might otherwise not have had. 'It isn't what I want.'

Suddenly, much to the surprise of both Sandra and me, Yvonne burst into tears, then told me, between sobs, 'You can't imagine how much you've hurt me. I wish you would change your mind. I can't go back to the office and tell my manager that you don't want me to work with you. Won't you reconsider, Zoe? Please.'

But when I still said 'No,' the tears stopped as abruptly as they'd started and Yvonne's tone changed completely as she snapped at me, 'Well, you won't get Susie' – who had been my key worker while I was at Denver House – 'if that's what you're hoping for.' Then she snatched up her handbag, scowled at us both and stormed out of the house. Which was a bit shocking, but at least made me feel vindicated for not wanting her to be involved in any way with my future life.

I had just turned 17 when I left the foster home and moved into supported housing, which was a two-bedroom house that I shared with a lad who was about the same age as me. I don't know if they'd do that today – put a vulnerable teenage girl in a house where the only other occupant was a lad and where a key worker came in for just 20 or 30 minutes a day. Maybe they wouldn't normally have done it *then*, but no one had bothered to check my files and read my history. If they had, they'd have realised I needed a lot more support. At the time, it felt as though the care system had simply washed its hands of me.

I didn't really like the idea of sharing a house, even with a lad who seemed to be okay and was hardly ever there. But my experience of fostering hadn't turned out the way I'd hoped and I didn't want to go into another residential home like Denver House, so I knew things could have been worse. Suddenly though, after living in a house full of noisy kids, I found myself surrounded by silence, sitting alone for hours on end, struggling to look after myself, and spending all the money I was given every week, not on heating, electricity, food, service charge and the other bills it was intended for, but on alcohol.

When you've lived with other people all your life – even people who've been horrible to you – it's a very frightening experience to find yourself on your own and responsible for doing things you don't know how to do and can't see the point of anyway, because the one thing you *do* know is that you aren't going to end up anywhere you would want to be.

My key worker, a woman called Helen who worked for the housing association that provided the accommodation, came to see me every day and was supposed to teach me 'independent living skills'. And although she did show me how to work the heating and taught me how to cook a couple of basic meals, why would I want to go to all the trouble of making a pasta bake, eat it, and then sit staring at the walls feeling miserable when I could spend the money on whisky and not feel anything at all? So I drank. Then the heating got shut off – during a very cold December – and my leaving care worker, a well-dressed woman in her mid-thirties called Delia who had been allocated to my case after I'd said that I didn't want Yvonne and who also visited me occasionally, ended up some months later having to sort out all the bills I hadn't paid.

I was already studying for A levels at the sixth-form college when I moved into the house, and I found it increasingly difficult to motivate myself when I was living on my own. The fact that I had almost no social skills didn't help, because I didn't know how to behave with the other students in a way that would have enabled me to fit in. Looking back on it now, I realise I was depressed – as I was for most of my teenage years. So after a while I stopped going in to college and eventually they sent me a letter saying that as they assumed I'd left, they had cancelled my place.

I had told Helen I was gay, and apparently she'd told the manager of the house – who was a relative of hers – that she'd watched TV with me in my room, allowed me to drink alcohol and given me her personal phone number. Then, one day, when I hadn't been in to college for about a month, she told me, 'I'm really sorry, Zoe. I told her in confidence, but I'm afraid they're going to ask you to leave the house.'

A couple of days later, I had a meeting with my social worker and the house manager, who said, 'It's to protect the staff – and yourself,' although she didn't say what from.

Sandra used to say that I wasn't fostered, I was family. But although that clearly wasn't true, I'd got used to living in the foster home and had been surprised by how lonely I felt and how difficult I found it being on my own. So although I didn't want to go back into a residential home, at least I would be living with other people again. It didn't really matter by that time anyway: when you've lived in the sort of places I'd lived for a few years and you know you're not wanted in your own home and don't belong anywhere else, there's not much of your soul left for anyone to stamp on.

Chapter 15

There were six other residents – one girl and five lads – living in Highfield when I moved in, and a constantly changing staff who came in to do the morning shift, the evening shift and the waking night shift. It was a large, three-storey Victorian house, with steps up to a solid wooden front door and with a tiny yard beyond the kitchen that led into a cobbled back passage. Whoever had chosen the paint colours seemed to have done their best to ruin it, however, as the walls of the hallways and up the stairs were painted a hideous orange, which seemed slightly less horrible when compared to the purple walls of the dining room, which clashed horribly with the green carpet that covered half the floor and was identical to the carpet at Denver House. There were other similarities between the two places too – both had mismatched utilitarian furniture, for example. But the rooms at Highfield were slightly bigger and a bit less cramped, the mattresses on the beds were better, and the living room on the first floor had a high ceiling and a big bay window that made it feel light and spacious.

Highfield was, in effect, a children's home for 16- to 18-year-olds, although, because of our ages, we were expected to live more independently than I'd done at Denver House. Although we had to buy most of our own food, breakfasts were provided and I was quite proud of the fact that after I'd been living there for just a few days, I persuaded the manager to add more options to the weekly list of provisions we had to choose from – which made me popular with the other kids too!

Everyone had a cupboard in the kitchen, which you had to remember to lock or someone would pinch whatever you put in it. There was no lock on the communal fridge/freezer, however, although fortunately there was a little fridge in every bedroom, so after the first couple of days I kept my sandwiches and any other bits of food I bought in there.

You don't talk to anyone about anything that matters in a place like that, certainly not in the early days when you're trying to fit in, and I spent most of the time in my room for the first few days, as I'd always done, until Lizzie, the other girl who lived there, invited me to have a drink and a smoke with her. I often sat in her room with her after that first time, and eventually we started talking to each other about our families and how we'd ended up in care.

The other friend I made after I'd been at Highfield for a few days was a 13-year-old girl called Mia, who I met in a local park. She'd gone there for the same reason I had – to have a drink – and we ended up sitting on the grass together chatting. I didn't say much about myself, but she had just started to tell me about how unhappy she was living at home when a group of five men in their early twenties came over and offered us some cannabis, which, stupidly, we accepted.

The men had been talking to us for a few minutes when two of them walked away. Or, at least, I thought that's what they'd done, until I heard laughing and felt something hit my back and turned around to find that one of them was peeing on me. Feeling sick, I stood up and said, 'Come on, Mia. Let's go.' It felt a bit surreal for a moment, as if Mia was me at that age and I wanted to protect her so that she didn't have the life I'd had for the last four years. So when she said she was going to stay, I kept insisting, until eventually she got up and came with me.

Even though it was only the early evening, I walked all the way home with her before heading back to Highfield, and after telling her, briefly, about what had happened to me at Denver House, I added, 'So you need to watch out for yourself, and stay away from men like that.'

I didn't ever see Mia again, but she obviously didn't take my advice, because apparently she's in prison now, for killing a man like the men we walked away from that night.

While I was living in the foster home, someone who came for just a couple of days left a mobile phone when they moved on, and Sandra said I could have it. I'd given the number to Frances before I moved into the house where I'd lived for just a month, and she'd visited me there once. Then, when I was at Highfield, she phoned me one evening and asked if I'd babysit for her youngest child, a little boy who was 11 years old and who I'd met on one occasion at Denver House when she dropped in briefly and brought him with her.

The little boy was already in bed when Frances picked me up from Highfield and took me back to her house, and as she didn't have to leave for work immediately, she sat watching TV with me for a while. I don't remember what we were watching, but she made some comment about a woman having a 'typically lesbian hairstyle', then added quickly, 'Oh, sorry. I shouldn't have said that.'

I still hadn't told anyone except Paula and my key worker that I was gay, so I was embarrassed and wondered what she meant. Then, a few weeks later, I was summoned to a meeting with her manager and another woman who took notes while I was asked questions about our relationship, which I answered evasively because I was anxious not to say anything that might get Frances into trouble. There was no follow-up to the meeting, so I didn't really know what prompted it or what the point of it was. But although we spoke on the phone a few times after that, I never actually saw her again.

Looking back over my story now, I can see that I haven't really been able to explain the role Frances played in my life during those three years after I was first taken into care. I think the reason she seemed important at the time was because she was the only adult who tried to engage with me in any way. Maybe she was gay and recognised that I was. But she was much older than me, and I wasn't at all interested in her in that way. She was more like a mother figure – or what I imagined a mother figure to be – which is probably why I found it so hurtful when she veered between being nice and horrible to me. In the end, though, she didn't do me any favours: she just confused me and made me feel even worse about myself. Perhaps she had problems of her own. It's only now that I realise that isn't an excuse for the sort of erratic, manipulative behaviour she exhibited when it's your job to care for children who desperately need consistency and approval.

It's difficult to describe how I felt throughout that period of my life. I had given up and become resigned to the way things were because I really believed that nothing would ever change and that my life would always be the same, for however long it lasted before I eventually committed suicide. And when you feel like that, it's almost impossible to summon the mental or physical energy to do anything that might make things better.

For example, a condition of my residency at Highfield was that I attended an alcohol programme that was run during the day. However, because I was very depressed and all I wanted to do was sleep and drink, I found it very difficult to engage with it – or with anything else. So I was still putting myself at risk, asking people to go into shops and buy alcohol for me.

Not long after I moved in, a guy who agreed to take the money I offered him and buy me a small bottle of whisky came out of the shop with a carrier bag containing the bottle I'd asked for and a much bigger one. 'You can have the big one if you share the small one with me,' he said. So I went with him to a house around the corner from the shop, where we sat on the floor of his room and drank it.

The next thing I knew, two police officers had burst into the room, where I was lying on the bed naked from the waist down, with no memory of anything that had happened. Apparently, one of the neighbours had dialled 999 because she heard screaming, and after I'd scrabbled around on the floor to find my clothes and put them on, I gave the police officers my name and address and they took me back to Highfield.

I never heard any more about that incident, so I don't know if the police followed it up with the man who'd bought the whisky. Probably not.

A few days later, I was given a verbal warning about not taking part in the alcohol programme. I did go to it, in fact, just not as often as I was supposed to. So I don't know if it would have done any good if I'd gone to every session. Maybe not, because I don't think I was ready for a programme of any sort after everything I'd gone through and without the one-to-one support I really needed. For me, drink was the only thing that ever made anything better – or at least seemed to, because in reality it was actually making everything far worse.

There were several men who used to park opposite Highfield and drive alongside me as I walked down the road. I just kept walking and pretended I couldn't hear them telling me to get into their cars. But after one of them threatened to kill me if I ignored him again, I started asking a member of staff to go with me to the shop. Even that didn't deter the men, however, and on at least a couple of occasions when I was with someone, they drove slowly beside us asking us to go for a drive with them. 'Don't acknowledge him. Don't look at him,' the member of staff said as we hurried back to the house. But I could see she was shocked and shaken by it.

I was afraid of the men too, but I'm ashamed to say I didn't always ignore them. Sometimes, I'd tell one of them that I was on my way to buy alcohol and if he offered to buy it for me, I'd let him give me a lift. The truth was, I was drinking even more by that time and didn't really care what I had to do to get it. Being abused had become a way of life for me and as I couldn't see any way out of it, I thought I might as well try to get some advantage from it. Then, one day, my friend Lizzie was attacked and raped in a park just down the road, which made me think again about what I was doing.

A few weeks after Lizzie was attacked, we were walking

back to Highfield together when a man drove past us very slowly, obviously trying to get our attention. At first, we just ignored him, then Lizzie suddenly grabbed my arm and whispered, 'It's him! That's the man who raped me.' And when I glanced towards the car, I realised to my horror that it was a man called RJ, who I sometimes went with willingly because he supplied me with alcohol.

'Run!' I said to Lizzie, and we darted down a side road, where we waited until we were certain he wasn't following us, then ran back to the house. 'But he knows where I live,' I told her when we'd caught our breath. 'He's got the payphone number here.' Then I explained how I knew him, before adding, 'I won't see him again though, now that I know what he did to you.'

We did tell the staff about RJ and they told the police, but they never caught him, and eventually he stopped phoning the payphone and threatening to kill us.

Because I was drunk most of the time, I didn't have the judgement required to avoid getting myself into danger-ous situations, or the ability to extricate myself once I was in them. So when I met a man who went into the shop to buy alcohol for me on several occasions without asking for anything in return, it felt as though I'd found a friend at last. He said his name was Logan, and after a while, when I began to feel that I could trust him, I gave him my phone number when he asked for it and he'd send me texts when he was in the area, then we'd sit in his car and drink the alcohol he'd bought for me at the shop.

One day, I told him I was gay, and he said he didn't mind. Then the next time I saw him he said, 'I've got a friend who's gay. I could introduce you to her if you like. It's a shame though. If you were straight, you could have moved in with me.'

When I laughed and answered, 'No thanks to both propositions,' he pulled a fake hurt expression, then he laughed too and said, 'Well at least let me take you to a party tomorrow. It might go on quite late, so maybe you should tell the staff some story about where you're going and give a fake address. Then we can stay as late as we like without them reporting you missing to the police.' So, the next day, I wrote down the address of a friend from school and told a member of staff I was going to stay the night with her.

The house where the party was being held was about 30 minutes' drive from Highfield and there were four or five men and a girl of about my age there when we arrived. The girl seemed really nice and I was chatting to her when Logan said we had to leave. 'But why?' I asked him. 'We've only been here for about half an hour and I've only had one drink. You said it was going to go on late.' He wasn't really listening though, and the next thing I remember I was in the passenger seat of his car and he was on top of me.

As the world slowly came back into focus, I saw that he had his penis in his hand, then realised that my underwear and trousers were around my thighs and I couldn't move. It was obvious that nothing was going to stop him and I

remember repeating, 'Use a condom. Use a condom.'
Then everything went blank again, until I woke up at
4 o'clock in the morning, still in the passenger seat of his
car, with my underwear and trousers on. He had parked
just up the road from Highfield, and he didn't say anything
as I got out and walked away.

When I got back to the house, there was a police car
outside and I can remember thinking as I let myself in and
tiptoed past the office that all I wanted to do was go to bed
and sleep. But when a member of staff called to me, I went
in. Although it turned out that the police were actually
there about another matter that had nothing to do with
me, one of the officers told me to sit down and started
asking me questions about where I'd been, who I'd been
with and what I'd been doing. Then someone tut-tutted
and said, 'Look at the state of her,' obviously without
having any concern for me at all, as if she thought I had
deliberately set out to make such a horrible mess of
my life.

Even though I'd only had one drink that night, I zoned
out and didn't answer when they asked me if I'd had any
alcohol or had 'taken anything'. So eventually they told
me I could go to my room, where I passed out on the bed.

It was only when I woke up the next morning that I
realised my underwear was on back to front and my body
was covered in bruises. It was obvious that I'd been
drugged, although when I told a member of staff
everything I could remember about what had happened,

she just shrugged as if to say, 'What do you expect?' So I went back to my room and tried to shut it out of my mind.

I didn't see Logan again. But about five weeks later, I discovered I was pregnant.

I was terrified as soon as I realised I'd missed a period, and when I told Lizzie, we went into town and she stole a pregnancy testing kit for me. Then, back in my room a few minutes later, we watched in horror as a cross appeared on the screen.

'It can't be right,' Lizzie said. 'You must have done something wrong. You'll have to do it again.'

So she went back into town, to a different shop, and stole another one. And when that was positive too, I told a member of staff, who made an appointment for me to see a doctor the following day.

It felt surreal, like watching something that was happening to someone else, when the doctor confirmed that I was pregnant and booked me in to have an abortion. No one asked me how I felt about being pregnant or what I wanted to do, and there was no mention of any options. And because I felt so detached from it all, I just allowed them to make all the decisions and didn't ask any questions.

I'll never forget the day I had the termination. I still have nightmares about it, and still feel a terrible sense of guilt and shame, as well as a lot of anger because things could have been very different if I'd been given some support. Even though my pregnancy was the result of rape, and I know I wasn't in any fit state to raise a child myself, I hate the thought that the baby – who would be a child of 12 now – wasn't given the chance to live and be adopted by parents who would have loved him or her. I won't ever forgive myself for that.

I never accepted another lift after I'd had the abortion, and not long afterwards I decided to go back to college. First though, I had to choose some courses, so I spoke to an adviser at the college who told me, 'What you *ought* to be studying is Health and Social Care with Religious Studies.' I suppose he thought that, being in care myself, I'd have an insight that would enable me to help other kids in similar situations. And maybe he was right. But it wasn't what I wanted to do, although, unfortunately, I didn't have enough confidence to say so, and it wasn't long after I'd enrolled to study the subjects he suggested that I realised I hated them.

About a month after I started studying again I turned 18, and on the night of my birthday Lizzie and I went out to celebrate. We both had a lot to drink during the evening and when we got separated somehow, I decided to walk back to Highfield on my own. It should only have taken me about 20 minutes, and I don't know long I'd been walking when a man suddenly appeared and tried to drag me off the street. He took me completely by surprise, and maybe it was because I was so startled that I managed to fight him off and get away. When I got back to Highfield, I went straight up to my room without stopping at the office to say hello the way I normally did, and ignored a member of staff who tried to speak to me.

Just after lunch the next day, one of the deputy managers came to find me and said she needed to talk to me about something serious. 'The police phoned,' she said, after we'd gone into the office and she'd closed the door. 'They say a girl who matches your description was seen on CCTV last night struggling to get away from a man who dragged her behind the library, out of sight of the camera. They're worried in case he sexually assaulted her. So, was it you, Zoe? If it was, it's something you should report.'

I had no memory of being dragged behind the library. I just remembered struggling when a man tried to pull me down the street, then running as fast as I could when I managed to get away. So I said it wasn't me and that I didn't know what she was talking about, because I was ashamed that I'd been drunk and because the fact that something like that had happened on what should have been a special birthday made me wonder if anything good would ever happen to me, which was a possibility I didn't want to think about.

Within days of that incident, after chewing me up for the last five years, the care system finally spat me out and I moved into a flat to live on my own.

I don't think the transition would be as abrupt today. In fact, what I didn't know at the time was that it shouldn't actually have happened the way it did, not least because I was probably less able to look after myself at 18 than I had been when I was first placed in care five years earlier.

I hadn't gone home on many visits during the time I was living at Highfield. When I did, my mum was still violent and nasty, my dad still made lewd comments, and it began to dawn on me that they were never going to change. As I discovered later, I wasn't the only person who had reached that conclusion: my leaving care worker and the social worker I had at that time stated in one of their reports that contact with my family was detrimental to my well-being, although, paradoxically, they also said it was a good thing that my flat was so close to my home.

Having lived in care for several years, you might think it would be nice to have my own place. But the flat was just somewhere social services put me and I didn't feel safe there, mostly because, in my mind, it was still connected with the care system that had let me down so badly and so repeatedly. I didn't have any say in it though; it was just a case of, 'This is what we've found for you. This is where you're going to be living.' And although I suppose I was lucky to have *somewhere*, it was the sort of dismal flat on the first floor of a run-down semi-detached council house that made you think of that saying, 'Abandon all hope, ye who enter here.'

The previous tenant must have been a very heavy smoker, judging by the yellow nicotine stains on some of the walls, and the whole place was badly in need of redecorating. There was damp in the flat too, so some of the plaster was crumbling off the walls; none of the windows shut properly, and most of the furniture – which looked as though it had been left over from a sale at a charity shop – was broken and/or had graffiti all over it.

There were two flats in the house and the old guy who lived in the one downstairs seemed a bit weird, although I didn't ever really speak to him. We each had access to half the garden and I was told that the council would clear my half before I moved in, which was a relief because it was so overgrown with brambles and weeds you couldn't even see the paving stones underneath it all. It wasn't cleared though, and after I'd been living in the flat for a while, I started getting letters from the council telling me that one of the terms of my tenancy agreement was that I must keep my half of the garden tidy, which felt like yet another responsibility I didn't want and couldn't cope with. I did do it in the end, however, despite the fact that I didn't ever use the garden.

Nothing changed after I moved into the flat. The vicious circle just continued: I was lonely, so I drank; when I was drunk, I became an easy target for abusive men; when I was abused, I felt even more distressed and lonely; so I drank …

I was getting about £45 a week in state benefits, a minimal amount of which I spent on food and the rest went on alcohol, which meant there was nothing left over to pay my bills. The problem is, when you drink enough for long enough, it takes longer to achieve the deadening effect that used to come quite quickly. So you have to start drinking earlier in the day to try to shut down your conscious mind before the dark thoughts have a chance to get a grip.

I hated living on my own there. Every minute of every day was a struggle. So much so, in fact, that I started going home again just so I didn't have to be on my own for 24 hours a day, seven days a week. Even being with my parents, who often didn't speak to me at all and who I knew didn't want me in their house, was better than being alone in an unheated flat.

Going home was a chance to get something to eat too, although Mum would make me beg for a sandwich and then didn't always give me one. When she did, she would sometimes serve it to me on the tin plate she used to force me to go to the toilet on when I was a little girl, and when I asked her to use a different plate, she just sneered and said, 'Beggars can't be choosers.' And even though she was happy to supply me with drink, she also refused to give me any money for my gas meter. In fact, she thought it was funny I was in such dire straits, and on the one occasion when she came to the flat, she laughed when she saw how dismal it was and that it was so cold you could see your breath in the freezing air. She'd brought a little thermometer with her and she was grinning when she showed me the reading, which was in the red zone below zero. 'You wouldn't be in this situation if you'd kept your mouth shut,' she told me again. 'It's only what you deserve.' And I believed her.

Eventually, despite the way my parents treated me, I started going home almost every day, because at least it was somewhere. I don't normally feel sorry for myself, but I can't think about that time now without getting upset when I remember how incredibly lonely I was. One day I was living in Highfield with other people, the next I was entirely on my own. Even if the 'care' I was receiving fell far short of what it should have been, at least there had been people there, and someone else had been responsible for all the practical things like providing heating, hot water and food. My key worker did sit down with me to work out a budget before I left Highfield, but what I really needed was someone to help me understand and deal with the reasons *why* I spent all my money on alcohol.

I felt ashamed that I didn't have any money to pay for an Internet connection or buy new clothes like most of the other students who lived with their parents could do. I was completely out of the loop at college, and just used to listen when they talked about what they were going to do at the weekend and where they would meet up on the Saturday night. So I was pleased when Frances got in touch with me again.

She rang and arranged to come to the flat a few times after that, and each time I would get excited at the prospect of having a visitor and someone to talk to for a while. But she didn't ever turn up, or let me know that she wasn't going to be able to make it, which made me feel even worse than I did before. Then, one day, she sent me a text saying, 'I can't do this anymore,' followed by a second message that was even more cryptic and said, 'It's all or nothing. I have to give you all or nothing. And I can't give you my all.' It didn't make any sense, and it was the last time I ever heard from her.

I was supposed to be going to college full-time, but not long after I moved into the flat I just gave up again. Then the college gave up on me too, and sent me a letter like the one I'd had before saying, 'As you have not attended for X days' – I can't remember how many days it was – 'we consider you to have left.' So then there was no reason for me to get out of bed at all, except to buy alcohol.

I can remember at around that time looking out of the window of the flat one day and thinking, 'Did all those things really happen to me when I was in care? What was the point of living through all that just to end up in a situation that's every bit as bad – maybe even worse – as the one I was in when it all started?' With no college work to do, no friends, and parents who didn't want me around, what was the point of any of it?

I did still have a care worker, but she was unsympathetic, and when she came to the flat one bitterly cold day and saw that there was no food in the cupboards, she told me, 'It's your responsibility to look after yourself now. If you choose to spend all your money on alcohol, you're the one that's going to have to deal with the consequences and sort it all out.' And because I didn't know *how* to sort it out, and was tired of being unhappy, I decided to kill myself.

Chapter 16

I had been prescribed antidepressants on numerous occasions but had never taken them regularly. A member of staff used to give me one every day when I was living in supported housing, then watch to make sure I swallowed it. Once I turned 18, however, I became responsible for getting and taking the tablets myself. I don't know how many I took that night, or how many drinks I'd had, and I don't have any memory of phoning my old foster carer Sandra, who must have phoned for an ambulance. I can't have taken many though, because I was only in hospital overnight.

It was Sandra who picked me up from the hospital the next morning too. She didn't say much as she drove me back to my flat. When we got there, she searched all the cupboards to make sure I didn't have any more tablets hidden away anywhere, then said goodbye and left, and I never saw or spoke to her again.

Although she hadn't commented on the fact that the flat was cold and the fridge and food cupboards were empty, she did apparently phone social services to tell them, 'Zoe's struggling'. But when my leaving care worker came round to check on me a few days later, she was critical rather than encouraging or sympathetic, telling me, in effect, that what I'd done was stupid, that I was an adult now and should behave like one. 'I've got younger children who are still in care who need me much more than you do,' she said irritably. 'So, in future, you're going to have to think twice before you contact me.'

Perhaps she thought my suicide attempt had just been attention seeking, and maybe she was right. But there are reasons why people feel the need to seek attention, and making them feel guilty and inadequate for not being able to manage the way adults are supposed to do is likely to do more harm than good. And, to be honest, I didn't feel like an adult at all. I think I'd stop maturing psychologically four or five years earlier, when I was 13, and I simply didn't have the mental capacity to deal with any of the things adults have to deal with. Unfortunately, it was a realisation that made me feel even more helpless and hopeless, although maybe I'd have been a bit less self-deprecating if I'd known then that a lot of the problems I was having are common amongst people who have experienced trauma of some sort.

I hated being on my own all the time when I was in the flat. Sometimes, though, you *do* need to be careful what you wish for, because one day Keith – the boy who had been adopted by Sandra and Bill and had sexually abused Rachel – turned up at my front door. I think Sandra must have given him my address, and it was stupid of me to let him in, knowing what I knew about him. But I was so surprised to see him standing there when I went downstairs and opened the front door of my flat that I didn't really have time to think of an excuse.

He didn't seem to realise that I wasn't exactly delighted to see him though, and his attitude was friendly as he told me, 'I was just passing and thought I'd come and say hello. So … Can I come in?' I wanted to say no, but for some reason didn't feel as though I could. So I opened the door wider and he went ahead of me up the stairs.

I'd been trying really hard not to drink alcohol since the suicide attempt, but I asked if he'd like a glass of juice, and I had just turned away from him to go into the kitchen when he grabbed me from behind, put his arm round my neck and pulled me backwards, pressing me against his groin. My immediate instinct was to try and fight him off, but I froze when I realised he was aroused. Then, trying to keep my voice steady so he wouldn't know how scared I was, I asked him what he was doing, and when he didn't answer, I told him to take his hands off me.

When he still didn't say anything or release his grip, I tried to pull away so that I could turn around and face him. But he just tightened his hold on me, then dragged me backwards across the living room and pushed me down on the sofa – *my* sofa, in *my* living room, in *my* home. As my fear turned to anger, I struggled to fight him off, but he was much stronger than I was, and after throwing himself on top of me, he forced my legs apart, pinned my hands above my head and started trying to pull down my jeans.

As I couldn't move my legs, I concentrated on trying to loosen his grip on my hands, and when I eventually managed to wrench them free, he started grabbing at my chest and trying to kiss me. We seemed to have been tussling and fighting for a long time, although it can't have been more than a few minutes, when he suddenly stood up, pulled up his trousers, sat down in the chair opposite the sofa and asked, as if nothing had happened, 'So how are you, Zo? Do you like living in this place?'

'I'm fine,' I answered, sitting up and buttoning my jeans. 'The flat's fine too.'

'Well, that's great,' he said. 'Sorry I can't stay longer, but I've got to go.' Then he stood up and walked down the stairs and out of the front door, which I locked firmly behind him.

Ten minutes later, when I was certain that he'd gone, I left the flat, walked round the corner to a shop and bought a 3-litre bottle of cider.

It wasn't until I got back to the flat that I caught sight of myself in the mirror and saw the bite marks on my neck. The whole incident had been humiliating and horrible, but maybe the worst thing about it was the shame I felt when I realised that everyone in the shop had seen the marks too. Bursting into tears, I picked up the bottle of cider, then crawled into bed to drink it.

I was having some counselling at that time, which had been arranged for me by the leaving care team. The problem was, I don't think the counsellor had much experience of dealing with the sort of things I talked about, and because she didn't seem to know how to respond, I found it difficult to engage with the sessions. However, I did tell her about the incident with Keith, and when I showed her the bite marks on my neck, she gave me some antiseptic cream, and never mentioned it again.

Sadly, it was only the bad things like Keith's assault that marked the passing of the days, weeks and months while I was living in the flat. Most of the time, I stayed in, drinking and sleeping, or, when I couldn't bear to be alone for a minute longer, visited my parents. I'd been living like that for almost a year and had just turned 19 when my dad died.

One of my parents' neighbours rang to tell me Dad had had a heart attack. 'The ambulance men are still working on him,' she said. A few minutes later, I was standing in the living room of my parents' house watching the paramedics use paddles to try to start his heart, while Mum stood in the hallway, crying and saying, to no one in particular, '*Do* something.'

When they carried Dad out of the house on a stretcher, one of the ambulance men told me not to look, and I can remember thinking, 'Don't tell me what to do.' So I did look, which is when I realised that I must have just watched my father die, because although they didn't say he was dead, I knew they would have secured his head on the stretcher if he was still alive.

Mum clung to me, sobbing and shaking, while they put Dad in the ambulance, which felt strange because it was the first time she had ever touched me when she wasn't angry. What really surprised me, however, was that I didn't feel sorry for her at all, because I knew she was only concerned for herself, as she always was. What I wanted to do was shake her off and say, 'Don't cling to *me* for comfort. What have you ever done to try to comfort me?' I didn't though. I went with her to the hospital, where we were met by Jake, Ben and Michael. And then she didn't need me anymore.

Later that day, we were driving away from the hospital in a taxi when Jake asked Mum, 'Should Zoe come home with us?'

'No. She'll be all right,' Mum said. So they dropped me off at the flat on their way, which made me feel as though they'd slammed a door in my face to shut me out, even though I don't know if I'd have wanted to be with them that night any more than they wanted me to be there.

Mum had had a health scare herself a few months before Dad died. I didn't know the details, but whatever had happened must have really scared her, because she'd given up drinking. So she was sober when I went to see her the next morning, although it was difficult to tell at first, because of the way she was wailing and crying. Ben was there too, trying to sort out some of the paperwork Dad didn't ever put into files, and it soon became apparent that what was really worrying Mum was how she was going to manage financially with Dad gone when she'd never had to pay a bill in her life. What was also obvious was that no one really wanted me there, so I only stayed for a few minutes, then went back to the flat and had a drink.

I feel incredibly sad about it all now. At the time, however, I think my overwhelming feeling was relief at the thought that I was no longer going to have to endure Dad's horrible gestures and sexual innuendos, which he was still making the last time I saw him, a few days before he died.

The funeral had to be delayed for a couple of weeks while Ben tried to sort out probate and release some money from Dad's bank account to pay for it. There were quite a few people there when it did eventually take place, including Ian, the son from his first marriage, and several members of his family who he saw regularly but who we'd had very little contact with over the years.

I was dreading the funeral, because I knew it was going to be one of those days when you just have to grit your teeth and get through it, and it proved to be every bit as difficult as I'd imagined it was going to be, partly because of the way my nan behaved. Nan was Mum's mum and didn't even like my dad, but she insisted on travelling with us in the family car from the house to the crematorium, which meant there was no room for Ian, so he had to go in the hearse with the coffin. Then, during the service, Mum sat with Jake and Michael on the first pew, and just as Ben, Ian and I were about to sit down in the one behind them, Nan pushed in front of Ian, so he ended up being squashed at the end of a pew that was meant to seat three people, while I was wedged in next to her, which made me feel really angry.

Although Ian hadn't had a great deal of contact with Dad when he was very young, the father he'd known was obviously very different from the one Jake, Ben, Michael and I had grown up with, and Nan kept poking Mum in the back then pointing at Ian because he was crying.

Of all the things that made me angry and upset that day, one of the worst was remembering something Dad had told us not very long before he died about getting on a bus and seeing Nan sitting there with a friend. 'She looked straight at me,' he said. 'So there was no question about whether she'd seen me. But she didn't even acknowledge me.' Now, there she was at his funeral, elbowing her way into something that didn't really concern her at all. That was what she was like about everything though, and she'd always had a lot of control over our family.

In fact, Nan had done a lot of things I had never been able to understand. And about three months after Dad's funeral, when I started challenging Mum and asking her questions I'd never have thought to ask her before, some of those things began to make more sense. That was when

Mum told me that Granddad – her own father – had sexually abused her when she was a child, starting from when she was nine and escalating after she reached the age of 12.

Hearing about the things he'd done to her made me feel protective towards her, like I used to feel when Dad was being horrible to her. But although it explained some of her behaviour as an adult, it didn't excuse all of it. Suddenly, all the disturbing and previously inexplicable memories *I* had of the things my granddad had done to me when I was a small child began to make sense too. But when I asked Mum why, knowing what he was like, she'd let me go to their house on my own, she just shrugged as if to say, 'This isn't about you.'

What was even more distressing to me than the revelations about what Mum's dad had done to her was her admission that she'd lied about the creepy things she used to tell me *my* dad had done – sniffing my underwear, for example, or watching me while I was asleep. 'I was the one who moved things in your bedroom,' she said, laughing as if she was telling me some really funny joke.

'But I don't understand,' I told her, feeling sick as it began to dawn on me that when Dad did start to make sexual comments to me, she had encouraged him, and that, horrible as they were, making those comments was all he had ever really done. 'Why?' I asked her again.

'Oh, you were such a *happy* little girl,' she answered spitefully. 'You were always smiling and cheerful and I thought, "Why should *you* have a happy childhood when I didn't? Why should *you* get on with *your* dad when mine did that to me?" So when you went to live at that care-home place, I wanted you to know what it felt like to be unhappy and not fit in. I wanted you to suffer. How was I supposed to know you would be almost raped to death? It wasn't *my* fault.'

When you've been depressed for a while, you get to the point when you no longer feel any strong emotions, particularly if you self-medicate with alcohol, as I'd been doing for several years. But I was completely stunned and hurt by the words my mum was spitting at me, like a snake spewing venom.

There was a photograph that I used to like looking at that had been taken on my first birthday. I was sitting on my brother Ben's knee, pointing at a cake in the shape of the number 1 that had my name written on it in pink icing. I think the reason I liked that photo so much was because it seemed to be evidence of a time when my parents must have cared about me enough to have had a special cake made to celebrate my birthday. I can't remember now if I mentioned it after Dad died or if Mum did, but when the subject did come up, for whatever reason, she told me, 'Your dad had that cake made specially for you by someone he worked with.' Then she laughed and added, 'I made sure he never did *that* again!' She obviously only said it because she knew it would upset me, and she was right: knowing the truth dispelled any idea I might have had that she had ever cared about me, and broke my heart because it was proof that my dad *did*.

There was still one tangible reminder of something nice I'd done with my dad when I was a little girl. But when I asked Mum if I could have the tape he'd recorded of me singing nursery rhymes when I was four years old, there was an expression of smug satisfaction on her face as she said that it was one of many things she'd thrown away after he died.

She told me much more over the next few weeks, and every story made me wonder which was worse, the effect her actions had had on me as a child, or the fact that she had quite deliberately destroyed my relationship with the father I used to love and who was now dead, so it was too late for any of the damage she'd done to be put right. When I got upset about it, however, she just shrugged and said, 'I never loved you and I wanted to destroy you,' as if she thought it was a perfectly reasonable explanation.

All the things Mum talked about during the weeks after Dad died made me think again about quite a lot of incidents that had previously seemed inexplicable. Like the recurring nightmare Ben told me he'd had after I'd been taken into care, for example, in which he was standing on the back doorstep of our grandparents' house, frantic because he couldn't move and save me from the monster that was doing horrible things to me in Granddad's shed. Maybe it wasn't just a random nightmare after all; maybe he'd seen or heard something that was related to the flashbacks I'd started having before I went to live at Denver House.

Not everything Mum told me was about my father or hers, however, and I can remember her laughing as she related the story of how, when I was three years old, I'd come out of my bedroom clutching a toy in each hand and she'd said, 'You can't walk down the stairs like that. You'll fall.'

'I'll be okay,' I apparently replied. 'I can do it.' So she'd stood and watched as I stepped cautiously from one stair to the next.

'You almost made it,' she told me. 'You were about four stairs from the bottom when you fell. You took quite a tumble.' She laughed again at the memory of it. 'Then you picked up your toys and I knew you were trying not to cry. But you see, I was right. I said you couldn't do it. I knew you'd fall.' She said it in the same tone of voice another mother might use to relate an anecdote about something clever or funny their child had done. But it was *her* cleverness she was recalling, for knowing better than a three-year-old, and the 'funny' bit was me falling down the stairs and hurting myself.

I already knew Mum has no empathy and that although she gets very angry when anything bad happens to *her*, she doesn't seem to be capable of feeling sorry for anyone else. I suppose that's why she genuinely didn't understand why I was so shocked when she said things like, 'I used to love going to visit my nan and granddad when I was a child.

They had a pond in their garden and I'd sit beside it catching frogs and squashing them.' Which explained why she'd got so angry with me a few weeks earlier for rescuing three little frogs I'd found at the side of the road outside her house, and had shouted at me, 'What did you do that for? There's something wrong with you.'

Another of the stories she told me was about one Sunday when Dad came home from the pub drunk – as he always was – and persistent in his sexual demands. I was living at Denver House at the time and had been home for a visit the previous day. So she decided to pay him back by getting him to phone and tell the member of staff who answered that he knew my period was about to start and just wanted to check that they would provide me with everything I needed.

She grinned as she told me how he was too drunk to realise the implications of what he was saying. But I could feel my cheeks burning with humiliation at the memory of what must have been that same day, when someone at the unit asked me if anything had happened during my visit home that could have made my father aware that I was expecting my period. I'd hated him for embarrassing me, when actually it had been my mother's idea to set him up and manipulate him in the hope of getting him into trouble – a score settled at my expense.

I think that was when I began to realise just how much she'd controlled and manipulated all of us, like some character in a novel or a film who sneaks around causing trouble and setting everyone against each other by dripping poison into people's ears.

From a selfish point of view, I found visiting Mum and hearing about how her father used to abuse her emotionally draining, and eventually it reached a point when I began to think, 'That's enough now. I can't take any more.' Knowing she'd lied about so many things made me angry and determined to fight back, and for the first time in my life I stopped blaming myself for everything that had happened. She had come very close to getting her wish and destroying me, but maybe there was still time for me to do something to help myself.

Chapter 17

After I'd joined the library when I was living at Denver House, I'd read a book called *You Can Heal Your Life*, by Louise Hay, which is a self-help book based on the idea that, 'What we think about ourselves becomes the truth for us ... Everyone is responsible for everything in our lives, the best and the worst. Every thought we think is creating our future.' Even during the worst times, I've always had an idea at the back of my mind of, 'This can't be it. It can't just finish like this.' So I'd found the book helpful, because it gave me something to think about, even though I wasn't in the right place mentally at the time to be able to act on any of it.

After listening to my mum's stories, however, and realising that she had quite deliberately done what she could to destroy my childhood and my relationship with my dad and make sure I didn't have the good life she felt she herself had been deprived of, I began to think it was time to take responsibility and try to fix my own life.

The first thing I did was join a library again. Then I started doing what the author Louise Hay calls daily affirmations, setting myself small targets such as, 'Today, I'm going to clean the cooker,' or 'This morning I'm going to get up, get washed and dressed and go to the shop to buy some bread and milk.' Before long, I had cleaned and redecorated the flat, bought some new furniture, and was beginning to wonder whether I might be able to do other things too, if I took everything step by step. So when I saw a sign advertising jobs at a local warehouse that was owned by a supermarket chain, I found out how to apply, then went to a charity shop and bought myself some clothes that I thought would be suitable to wear if, by some chance, I was asked to go for an interview.

I hadn't ever worked before, and although I was trying to think more positively, I still believed I wasn't really good enough. So I was surprised and quite nervous when I got an interview, and very excited when I was offered a job as a warehouse operative. It was a full-time job, which meant I was able to sign off benefits and, for the first time in my life, pay my own rent and council tax with money I'd earned myself, like any other normal adult would do.

Within days of starting work, there was food in my cupboards, money in the gas meter and the flat was warm. Then I threw away all the tatty clothes that had never suited me and all the shoes with holes in them that made my feet wet every time it rained, and bought myself some nice things that fitted me properly and that I wasn't ashamed to be seen in.

Even though I'd done well at school before the abuse and the alcohol made it so difficult to focus, I'd always been convinced I was too stupid to be able to do a proper job, so it was an amazing feeling to find that I could and to know that I was no longer dependent on benefits and didn't have to beg my mum for food. It's scary though, when I look back on it now, to think how close I'd actually come to hitting rock bottom.

It was hard work in the warehouse, with an early start on the days when I was doing the morning shift, and it didn't take me long to realise that I wasn't going to be able to keep it up unless I cut down on the drinking. I had been reliant on alcohol for so long by that time that the prospect of having to get through a day without it was daunting. But it actually proved to be less difficult than I'd expected now that I finally had something in my life worth being sober for.

I knew better than to expect Mum to be happy for me, of course. What I hadn't anticipated, however, was that the more independent and confident I became, the more she shut me out. Sometimes, she wouldn't answer the door when I went round to see her, and sometimes she flung it open when I rang the bell and shouted at me, 'Who do you think you are? You're not coming in. Go away.' All because she couldn't bear the fact that, despite her best efforts over the last 19 years, I was doing okay.

I went home less often after that, and started thinking about what *I* wanted to do. I don't think I'd ever previously thought that I might actually have a choice about what I did with my life, and when I started to think about it, I realised that what I really wanted to do was box. I know boxing is a controversial sport, but it *does* involve a lot of skill and I'd had a passion for it ever since I used to watch it on television as a little girl. What I also liked about it as I got older was the way it seemed to mirror the constant struggle to do better in life. But I knew that before I could even think about taking a boxing class, I was going to have to get fit. So, instead of sitting in the flat after I'd finished work for the day at the warehouse, I started swimming. Then I gave up smoking and took up running too.

I don't think I'll ever forget the first time I ran a mile without stopping. The fact that I could barely walk for two days afterwards seemed a price worth paying for the sense of achievement I had knowing I'd done something I'd never done before.

Alcohol was the last thing to go. I'd already cut down on it a bit, but I knew that if I didn't stop altogether, I would never get fit enough to do what I wanted to do. And anyway, now that my life had some purpose, I didn't feel lonely when I was on my own the way I used to do. It probably sounds daft, but it was as if I'd become connected to the rest of the world in a way I hadn't ever been before.

So even when I was alone in my flat, I didn't have the horrible sense of being totally isolated that I'd always had.

Perhaps it was because, for the first time in my life, I was just like everyone else: hurrying off to work, going for a swim, jogging through the park, and doing all the other normal things that normal people do. What I also began to realise was that using alcohol to dull your senses really *does* dull them, and I would sometimes stop to look at a flower and wonder why I'd never noticed before how bright the colours were. After having wished so many times that I was dead, it was an extraordinary experience to find myself appreciating being alive.

What also surprised me was the discovery that if I set my mind to doing something, I really could do it. I gave up drinking completely for three months, and although I did have an occasional drink after that – because I was having nightmares and flashbacks about the abuse I'd suffered when I was living in Denver House – I always limited it, because I had to be able to work and because I wanted to continue to do all the exercise I was doing.

Then, one day, as I was leaving the sports centre after swimming 30 lengths of the pool in the early-bird swim, I noticed a poster on the door advertising boxing classes at a gym that was just around the corner, and I remember thinking, 'It's on my way home. I might as well drop in.'

You often hear 'wellness gurus' and other people saying things like, 'Open your mind to new experiences and good things will happen,' which can sound a bit trite, because if it was as easy as that, why would bad things ever happen to anyone? But good things did happen for me after I started opening my mind to doing things I'd never have thought myself capable of doing. One of them was going to the gym that day and finding that a free class was just about to start – funded by a grant from the council – for people between the ages of 16 and 21. As I was 21, I joined it, then went back a couple of hours later to do another. And suddenly it felt as though I'd found the missing piece of a puzzle I hadn't even realised I'd been searching for.

After I'd done the second class, the teacher, who was a professional boxer, called me over and told me, 'Sometimes people just blow me away. They walk through that door and I think, "Where on earth did you come from?" Come back on Monday and I'll get the coach to have a look at you to see if I'm right and you've got what it takes.'

With the money I was earning at the warehouse, I'd been able to buy myself a second-hand bike, which I rode everywhere, and as I was riding it home through the park in the rain that day, a rainbow suddenly appeared in front of me, and when I reached out my hand, it looked as though one end of it was resting on my palm.

I sometimes use angel cards, which are a bit like tarot cards and can be a useful way of focusing your thoughts on a particular problem or question. I did them when I got home that day, and after shuffling the pack, the first card I picked out had a picture of a cloud on it and an angel holding a rainbow, with the word 'Study'. Again, I know some people will think it sounds stupid, but it made me feel as though I really was on the right track.

After I'd finished work the following Monday, I cycled to the boxing gym feeling very nervous, as though I was about to take part in the most important interview of my life. When I got there, the coach asked me to do some sparring to check that I didn't shy away from being hit. It's a stumbling block for some people, because as well as having a good technique when you're hitting an inanimate object, you need to be able to stand your ground and dodge the blows when a real person is trying to hit you in the face.

At the end of the session, the coach said, 'Okay, we'll train you. I think you might just have what it takes to become a professional.' And suddenly it was if someone had flung open every shutter and every door in a darkened room, filling it with almost blinding sunlight.

I had to pay for the classes, and fit them in around my shifts at the warehouse, but that was fine. I was earning enough money to cover the cost, and one of the many good things about the job I was doing was that my responsibility ended as soon as I walked out of the building, so I didn't have to worry about it at all.

I was running between 30 and 50 miles a week by that time – I could do a mile in six minutes – and I felt amazing. I got up at 4 o'clock every morning, thought about all the positives in my life while I ate my breakfast – that I was safe, had food to eat, a roof over my head and a job. Then, if I was on the early shift – from 6 a.m. till 2 p.m. – I trained for an hour or so before biking to work, went straight to the gym when I clocked off, and was on the treadmill by 2.30.

When I wasn't at work, running, swimming or at a boxing class, I was doing yoga or some other session at the sports centre. In fact, I was never at home, because setting fitness goals and achieving them had become an obsession. One day, for example, when I did a 13-mile run just fractionally over the time limit I'd set myself, I turned around and did it again. It took longer the second time, of course, because I was tired before I set out and because I'd almost run as far as I did in a week by the end of it. But I was so happy about the fact that I'd achieved something I'd never done before, I bought myself an ice-cream from the van that just happened to be in the park at the very spot where I ended my own personal marathon!

Looking back on it now, I realise I sometimes became stuck in a trap of everything having to be all or nothing. But it was the happiest time of my life in many ways. I rarely spoke to my mum. She wasn't interested in me at all now that my life was no longer a disaster, and without her entirely negative influence, my self-esteem was able to recover enough for me to start thinking about who I am, what I like and what I might be able to achieve if I put my mind to it. What I didn't realise, however, was that I wasn't just running to get fit: I was running away from all the bad stuff that had happened, stuff that I was going to have to deal with when it eventually caught up with me.

Chapter 18

I met Jess on an online dating site, then in person about a week later. I was 22, had never dated before and was very naive, still convinced that one day I'd find the 'special someone' I'd been waiting for since I used to sit under the stars on the roof at Denver House listening to Céline Dion singing about believing in your dreams.

I didn't trust people though, and when Jess rang about three weeks after we'd met up for the second time and said her husband had kicked her out and she wanted to move in with me, I cried when I put down the phone. It was a bit of a shock to discover she was married – she hadn't mentioned it in any of her emails or when we'd met. What really upset me, however, was the fact that I'd agreed to her coming to live with me because I thought it was my fault her marriage had broken down, but it wasn't what I wanted at all.

With work and boxing training going well, I'd decided I wanted to study counselling and fitness instructing, so that I could share the things that had turned my life around with other people who'd had similarly bad experiences. So, by the time Jess moved in – which she did with a carload of stuff the day after she'd phoned me – I'd cut back the hours I was working at the warehouse and had started going to college. Jess was working too, and for a while she commuted every day to a town about 40 minutes' drive away, close to where she'd been living with her husband.

Despite my initial misgivings, it wasn't long before I'd persuaded myself that Jess moving in to the flat had been a good thing. And then it all started going wrong.

It was my fault that I started drinking again. I didn't have to do it just because it was what Jess wanted to do. But although I know it sounds stupid, I think I was so anxious to have 'someone special' that I persuaded myself it was probably what everyone did with their partners when they fell in love, and went along with it. The problem was, just one drink when you're really fit can mess up your training, and with my history it had an effect almost immediately. The odd drink hadn't appeared to be a problem before I started boxing, but it wasn't ever just 'one drink' after Jess moved in, and it wasn't long before I was struggling, both mentally and physically.

Before I met Jess, I'd stopped relying on alcohol for the first time since I was 13 years old. And I'd done it myself, because the job and the boxing training had given me a reason to want to stay sober. But as any alcoholic will tell you, even with all the right kind of help and support, it's really tough to give up drinking. So I suppose, in the circumstances, the outcome was almost inevitable.

I won't go into all the details of what turned out to be a rather messy relationship that lasted, on and off, for a couple of years. Basically, we started bickering quite soon after Jess came to live with me. She needed more attention than I was always able to give her and got quite violent when she felt she wasn't getting it, and eventually it became impossible for me to do the work I had to do for college or to concentrate on anything. What made it worse was the fact that I was torn between thinking it was all my fault – after years of conditioning – and feeling guilty because I wished Jess hadn't come to live in my flat.

To be fit enough to do what I wanted to do, I had to train at the gym twice a day, and you have to be at the top of your game to do that. So if I'd been drinking with Jess or had had a late night, it had a very significant effect on my performance, and after a while I started to put on weight and go to the gym less often than I should have done.

Anyone who'd seen me when I was at rock bottom wouldn't have recognised the slim, fit, motivated, employed person I'd become by the time I met Jess. I had been proud of what I'd achieved and of the fact that I had done it all by myself. Now I was losing *everything*, and I didn't know how to claw it all back and re-focus on the positive things I'd fought so hard to build into my life.

While it was all falling apart, I kept telling myself, 'I can make this better,' which is what I used to believe about my relationship with my mum. So I should have known from experience that it wasn't going to work out. In fact, what I should have been telling myself was that Jess wasn't my 'special someone', however much I wanted her to be. I wasn't responsible for her and I should have just ended the relationship, picked up my own life and carried on. For some reason though, I couldn't do it; I couldn't let go. Perhaps it was because I'd never trusted anyone before and had always believed that, ultimately, everyone would let me down, so I couldn't bear to face the fact that, having finally allowed myself to become intimately connected with someone, I'd made a mistake.

After we'd battled on in the flat together for several months, Jess told me she was going home to her husband, and a few minutes later she'd gone. She came back after a couple of weeks though, then came and went several times after that, and every time she left it broke another tiny fragment of my heart, because I thought I really was in love with her.

I didn't ever tell Jess about what had happened to me at Denver House, just that I'd been in care and it hadn't been a great experience. I don't think I'd really faced it myself at that time. She used to talk about her childhood though, which had been traumatic for reasons that were mostly related to the mental health issues that had affected her mother and had eventually ended in tragedy.

246

What I hadn't realised was that although I'd been doing quite well on my own, working, going to college and doing the boxing training, and thought I was okay, I was actually still incredibly vulnerable and my self-esteem had only risen a notch or two above zero. So I probably would have fallen for almost anyone who had shown interest in me the way Jess had done. Maybe it was the fact that I'd allowed myself to get close to her emotionally as well as physically – which is something I still find incredibly difficult to do with anyone – that made me believe I must love her.

Despite everything that was happening with Jess, however, I did manage to get myself back on track and, after qualifying, got a job as a fitness instructor at a ladies-only gym. Everyone I worked with was really friendly and I loved my job. I was still doing the boxing training too, and was really enjoying working towards my goal of becoming a professional boxer.

After having an interview with the British Board of Boxing, I'd been given the initial approval I needed to be able to start the process of getting a licence to fight, which would also involve having brain scans and all sorts of other tests before I qualified and was able to start earning money from doing what I loved. I still couldn't believe that I was going to get the chance to do the one thing that had meant enough to me to enable me to turn my life around.

I had a couple of semi-professional fights at the boxing gym where I did my training – what they call white-collar fights, for people with little or no boxing experience – and although they'd both ended in a draw, at least I'd got my foot in the door.

Then Jess came back again and I started drinking even more, which led to me putting on weight and missing training sessions. I hadn't been to training for three weeks when I went to the boxing gym one morning and was told that I wouldn't be getting my licence after all. I was gutted, and more or less stopped going there altogether after that. So then I lost fitness, had to give up my job as a fitness trainer, and everything I'd built single-handedly out of nothing just vanished into thin air.

The one thing that did seem to stick with me after I'd lost everything else was the determination to work rather than fall back on benefits. I got two part-time jobs, one of them as a carer in a residential unit for adults with learning difficulties, which I really liked, except for the fact that I seemed to take all the problems of the people I was working with home with me every day. That's why I eventually gave it up and just did the other job, as carer to a lad called Tony, who was about the same age as me and who'd been born with a muscle-wasting illness.

Tony lived at home with his parents and younger sister, and my job was basically to get him up, washed and dressed and take him out in his wheelchair. I'd been working for the family for a few weeks when I started taking him to the gym. His mum, Evelyn, came with us the first time, but felt so embarrassed about not being fit she refused to come inside. It was partly because of the way she felt that day that she started going regularly to dance and fitness classes. Then Tony's very timid younger sister joined a karate class, which gave her confidence that transformed her almost overnight. And after I'd devised a very basic exercise programme for Tony, he eventually became fit enough to be able to stop taking some of the medication his mum thought he'd have to take forever.

It was amazing to see the change in Tony, not just in terms of what he could do physically or his increased ability to make eye contact with people, but also because of the calming effect exercise had on him. It was thanks to his mum's hard work and determination that he was already far more independent in the house than anyone had ever believed he could be. But nothing she had been able to do had had the effect that exercise had of reducing his sense of frustration, so that he stopped banging his head with his knuckles or biting his arm when he was upset.

Evelyn was very supportive of me too, when I was having problems because of Jess's comings and goings. But she could see that my own mental health was deteriorating because of it all, and eventually I had to give up that job as well. It was a very hard decision for me to make, and I still feel sad when I think about it. I knew I had to be honest with Evelyn though, and that it wasn't fair on Tony when I kept calling in sick and disrupting the routine he'd got used to and relied on. So I stopped working as a carer and got a part-time job in a factory.

Then one evening, when Jess had gone back – again – to live with her husband, two police officers turned up at my door and told me, 'I'm afraid we're going to need you to come down the police station with us. We've had a complaint from someone who says you've been harassing them.'

I knew immediately it was Jess, even though it didn't make any sense, because the few text messages we'd exchanged during the previous couple of weeks had all been amicable – 'How are you doing? I hope things are going well' – and she'd contacted me more times than I'd got in touch with her.

It was humiliating having to walk out of the house and get into a police car. The police officers were polite though, and apologised when we got to the police station, saying that because an accusation had been made, they had to go through the process of questioning me. So I told them about the text messages, they contacted the local police where Jess lived, then told me they wouldn't be taking it any further, and drove me back to the flat.

It was a horrible experience, but I forgave her, of course, and not long afterwards she came back – 'For good this time,' she told me.

I had just turned 25, and a couple of weeks later I got a letter in the post telling me to go for my first cervical screening test. I didn't make an appointment until almost a month later, and about a week after I'd been for the test, I got another letter saying that my results were abnormal and another appointment had been made for me. At the second appointment, they swabbed me with some dye, then used a camera to see if they could detect any abnormal cells, which, unfortunately, they could. 'Some of the cells are a bit irregular,' the doctor told me. 'So we need to do what's called a punch biopsy to find out what's going on. It sounds a bit daunting, I know, but it's just a small instrument that we use to extract a piece of tissue.'

All I could think about while he was talking was that it was cancer. So I didn't really hear what he said about the other things it could be, and by the time they'd done the test and I got home, I was feeling very anxious. My distress was nothing compared to Jess's, however, when I told her what had happened.

'I can't cope with this,' she said, bursting into tears. 'I can't lose you. Not after everything that's happened to me.'

'Well, it might not be anything serious,' I told her, trying to remember what the doctor had said. 'We won't know until they've got the results of the biopsy, which won't be until everyone goes back to work after the Christmas and New Year holidays. So I'm going to try not to worry about it till then.'

But nothing I said seemed to make her feel any better, and eventually I suggested she should talk to someone else about it. I didn't want to have anything to drink that night, so in the end Jess went out on her own, and when she came back, she was very drunk. I knew by that time that it was best not to say anything to her when she was in that state, although even saying nothing could make her suddenly go off the deep end and start accusing me of all sorts of bizarre and ridiculous things.

Unfortunately, however, the alcohol she'd drunk had transformed her self-pity into anger, and as I was feeling sorry for myself by that time, we ended up having a row, then wrestling like a couple of kids on the living-room floor.

I'd bought a little hamster during one of the periods when I'd been on my own in the flat, and when Jess kicked its cage a couple of times, then bent down to pick it up, I punched her. It was like an automatic reaction, and I was immediately sorry I'd done it. But she refused to speak to me when I tried to apologise and I could hear her crying as she went into the bathroom and locked the door. Although she slept on the couch that night, we talked about it in the morning, and after she accepted my apology, everything seemed to be okay.

We had another row a couple of days later – fuelled by alcohol, as they almost always were. Then Jess stormed off into the bedroom, and the next thing I knew, someone was ringing the bell and knocking very loudly on the front door.

It was 2 o'clock in the morning, so my first thought was that it was one of the neighbours coming to tell us to be quiet. In fact, it was two police officers, responding to a 999 call Jess had made from the bedroom saying I'd just punched her. It wasn't true, but as she still had the black eye I'd given her a couple of days earlier, I was arrested and taken to the police station.

Chapter 19

When we arrived at the police station, I told them I hadn't punched Jess and that I wasn't responsible for her black eye. 'Don't worry about it,' they said. 'She'll come round in the morning.' I had to spend the night in a cell though, and as they were closing the door I thought how stupid I'd been to have put so much effort into building a life for myself only to let it all slip away, leaving me right back where I'd been ten years earlier, sitting in a police cell. Only this time I *had* actually done what I was being accused of.

It surprised me sometimes that when it felt as though I was being torn apart by my emotions, my physical body continued to function normally, and as I lay on the narrow bed in that police cell, watching a small spider scuttling across the floor towards the door, I remember wishing that something would happen to stop my heart beating and my lungs inhaling and expelling air.

When the police took me back to my flat the next day and I found that Jess had packed up all her things and gone, I sat down and wrote a short story about the spider I had seen in the police cell.

Along came a spider

The human body is incredible. It amazed me to discover that no matter how much emotional pain is consuming you at any given time, the body still functions as it would normally. Your heart continues to beat. You continue to breathe. And your blood continues to deliver and distribute the oxygen that is needed to live, no matter how much you wish it didn't. Which begs the question, is there something deep inside us that keeps us going when the heart and mind long for an end to emotional suffering, for death?

I was locked inside a police cell at the time of my sudden realisation. I was sober. I had absolutely nothing to distract or numb me to the emotions that were tearing me to shreds, piece by piece, and then, along came a spider.

At first, I thought I had imagined it, the appearance of such a beautiful miracle – well, can you spin a web of silk? But I hadn't. It really was there. No longer was I alone in this cold cell. I had company.

I asked the spider why it was here and if it knew that it was inside a police cell, and I told it that, in my opinion, it was far too beautiful a creature to be in here.

'Why, that's just what I was about to say to you!' came the reply.

I was shocked, and explained how I had been arrested and that I had no choice in the matter.

'Of course you had a choice. There is always a choice,' the spider said.

I felt the first stirrings of anger as I recounted my story. I explained that I had been in a violent relationship for three years and that it had reached a violent climax, hence my arrest and detention.

'Why did you not leave this violent relationship sooner so that you avoided this, as you say, violent climax?'

I became defensive then, and shouted that it was because I had no choice.

'Why do you feel that you had no choice?' asked the spider again, calmly.

'Maybe I felt I had no choice because I felt I had no worth, no place or purpose. Maybe I felt I was not worthy of love from another and that I should be grateful for the little affection I did receive,' I snapped.

'Why?' asked the spider.

I sighed heavily, expelling all my anger. I could not stay angry at this beautiful miracle and my eyes filled with tears as I told it that at the age of 13, I was taken into care, and only three weeks later I was raped by

257

two men who had paid an older girl to pose as a friend and take me to their house. I told it how I was then introduced to another man who began to introduce me to lots of different men, and that I had been raped and forced to carry out sex acts on all of them. I told it how dirty I felt all the time and how the staff at the children's home never noticed that anything was wrong. I told it that I had cut myself just to feel something other than the sadness, shame and disgust that was forced upon me day after day, year after year. I told it how I became withdrawn and unable to socialise. I told it that I had let my ex-partner get closer to me than anyone had ever done before, and that what should have been pleasurable was painful to me, and how eventually I overcame that with her and so forgave the abuse in the hope of things getting better and through the fear of never knowing that intimacy again. Finally, I let myself cry and when I had finished crying, the spider spoke again.

'As you sit here in this cell, know that you too are a miracle, capable of miraculous feats. You have lived in darkness and fought with the devil and yet here you still are, talking to a spider and offering it kind words. Many would have seen fit to step on me, afraid of our differences, but you have embraced me in awe of them. The only time we have is now, and in this time we always have a choice, and there is no right or wrong. Do not weep over your choices. Take possession of them and strive to move forward, remembering that you, too, are a miracle!'

Then the spider made towards the cell door, where I noticed a tiny gap. It wasn't imprisoned after all.

'Wait!' I cried out, intrigued. 'Why are you here if you have been free to leave all along?'

'It's snowing outside and only a fool would refuse to seek shelter in a storm. And besides, I often like to visit the cells. It's amazing the kind of people you meet!'

I'd been told at the police station that I mustn't contact Jess, so I didn't, and I never saw or heard from her again.

A few days later, I got the all-clear from the hospital.

I don't know why Jess didn't drop the charge against me. Maybe, after her last accusation had proved groundless, she'd been told that she'd get into trouble for wasting police time if she didn't see it through on this occasion. Whatever the reason, she didn't 'come round' the next morning, and when the case went to court a couple of months later, I realised it had been stupid of me to lie to the police when they arrested me and say I hadn't been responsible for Jess's black eye, because it went against me when I explained at the court hearing what had actually happened.

I had Legal Aid, and a solicitor who turned up just half an hour before the hearing started, didn't seem to care if I ended up with a criminal conviction, and said, when I told him I wanted to defend myself against the charge, 'Forget about it. Let it go. If you challenge it and they find you guilty, you might have to spend time in prison.' So I pleaded guilty and was fined several hundred pounds, which I paid weekly out of the benefits I started claiming, because I didn't go back to work after that.

But at least I didn't have cancer. I'd told my mum about the biopsy while I was still waiting for the results, and she'd given me even less support than Jess had done. I don't know why I said anything, or what made me think she'd be sympathetic for the first time in my life. When I told her once that I was feeling suicidal, she'd said, quite seriously, 'Well, don't expect me to pay for your funeral. You'll have a pauper's grave.' I suppose I just kept hoping that one day she'd surprise me and say something nice.

After I gave up work, I just fell apart. I kept thinking about the spider in the cell at the police station and telling myself, 'You always have a choice. There's always something good to hold on to. You just have to find it. It doesn't matter what the police or anyone else thinks of you. You know who you are.' I didn't though: my drinking had got out of control again and after working so hard to establish an identity, I'd lost sight of who I was; all I could think about were the bad things that had happened.

I'd been told by a counsellor when I was 18 that, in her opinion, people didn't need antidepressants to overcome depression and anxiety and they shouldn't take them. So I wasn't taking any tablets at that time, and my depression got so bad I ended up spending almost every day in bed with the curtains closed, reading, drinking and eating bread and butter. I was 25, but felt as though I'd reverted to what I was like at 18; except that at 18 I hadn't yet had any opportunities to throw away like I'd just done with my job as a fitness trainer, the chance to box professionally, my own fitness ... Everything that had been important to me had turned to dust – or, more accurately, *I* had destroyed it myself – and I didn't think I would ever get any of it back again.

When Jess moved in to live with me in the flat, I had a desk in the bedroom, where I used to sit to do bits of writing, but I'd taken it to the charity shop after she said one day, 'You're not a kid. What do you want a desk for?' I'd taken down the inspirational quotes I'd stuck on the wall above it too, and got rid of various other things that had been important to me but that seemed childish when she pointed it out. What I didn't realise was that just the fact that those things mattered to me *made* them important, and by getting rid of them simply because someone else said I should, I was actually getting rid of bits of my own identity. And when I lost Jess, I no longer had the energy, or incentive, to try to get them back.

I see now that my relationship with Jess was doomed to failure before it even began. We both had problems, past and present, and were using each other: Jess needed somewhere to stay and didn't want to be on her own, and I was so lonely that I pinned all my hopes for the future on the first person who showed any interest in me and decided immediately that she was 'the one'. I'd never had a normal relationship with anyone, not even with my own parents, so I didn't understand about boundaries or what's acceptable, and what isn't.

The fall-out period after Jess, when I was drinking again and spending most of my time in bed, lasted for more than a year. I was depressed and really struggling, and had got to the point of not being able to cope anymore when I had an idea that made me think, 'If I do this, at least I'll end my life knowing I've done one thing that was worthwhile.'

During the time when I was working as a fitness trainer at the ladies-only gym, I'd devised a 12-week training programme I thought I could use at the boxing gym to help other women who'd been through traumatic experiences. All that remained to be done was for me to put it all together into some sort of coherent form, then find a way of making it available to the people who might benefit from it. I didn't know if it was going to be possible to do what I wanted to do, but suddenly I had something to focus on that was worth getting out of bed for.

It was after I'd started writing a business plan that I met Pam. I came across her website when I was looking for information about healthy eating, and when I saw that she does a lot of work in the community and is interested in helping people with various problems, I decided to contact her to see if some of the principles she's written about and some of the activities she's involved with could be incorporated into my training programme.

I was still very depressed – what I was really doing was trying to get things in order before I ended my own life – and I think that was clear to Pam when I contacted her and we spoke for the first time on the phone. I was feeling particularly miserable, so it was nice to be able to talk to someone. But because I rarely spoke to anyone, I had a sore throat for three days afterwards, which made me realise just how isolated I'd become. Then we met in person, and it felt as if she'd thrown me a lifeline just a fraction of a second before I drowned. She was in her late forties when we met, and as well as being sensible and sensitive in a very matter-of-fact way, she was really supportive when I started to open up and talk to her.

I had tried to get some support for myself before I met Pam, and my GP had given me a phone number and said I needed to refer myself to an alcohol service. But although I did two alcohol detoxes, they didn't work because I hadn't addressed the reasons *why* I was drinking. So then I referred myself to a counselling service for survivors of sexual abuse, and what became apparent during those sessions was that living so close to where all the bad things had happened was preventing me from moving forward with my life. Until I split up with Jess, I'd been repressing the abuse and all the horrible, inhumane things that had been done to me. But after I started going to counselling, the bad things were all I could think about.

The counsellor was already helping me to see that it wasn't my fault, and when I met Pam and she became my friend, she encouraged me to see that too, and eventually I began to feel that my life *was* worth fighting for.

It was Pam's idea that I should ask social services for my files. 'It would have been Children's Services that were responsible for your care at Denver House and subsequently,' she told me. 'And under the terms of the Data Protection Act, you have a right to see the records they kept about you. You've obviously got a lot of questions about what happened so maybe it would help you to have some answers. Think about it though. It has to be your decision. And bear in mind that you won't be able to un-know anything you discover.'

Pam lived about 50 miles away from the town where my flat was, and when I told her I'd decided to go ahead and apply for my files, she offered me a room in her very nice house, so that I wouldn't be alone while I was trying to deal with whatever I was going to find out.

Before I was allowed access to my files, however, I had to have a meeting with the records officer at a local council office, to see if I was 'strong enough' to be able to cope with what I might read. Pam went with me for the appointment, but when we got there I asked her to wait in reception, because it suddenly felt like something I wanted to do on my own.

'You've got a quite a story,' the records officer said. 'I'm a bit concerned that you might read things you don't know about that could be upsetting for you. So maybe, as well as redacting anything that relates to third parties, we should remove some of that information too.'

'I want to read it all,' I told her. 'Even the difficult bits. I feel that I need to know what happened so that I can finally have closure and draw a line under the time I spent in care.'

I think the fact that Pam had come with me and I wasn't alone helped to persuade her to let me read everything, except the redacted bits, and by the end of the meeting she'd agreed.

It was about a month after I'd first applied for my files that Pam and I went back to the council office to collect them. The woman who handed over the three big boxes to me said she knew Denver House and it wasn't a nice place to live. 'Just be thankful you didn't live there for a lot, a lot of years,' she told me, sounding so much like Cilla Black I had to repress the urge to release the tension that had built up inside me by saying something funny about it not having been 'a lorra, lorra laughs – Surprise! Surprise!'

I couldn't have thought of anything funny to say a few minutes later, however, when the records officer helped us carry the boxes out to Pam's car and I was sitting in the passenger seat, shaking and crying. I'd expected to be upset by what I would read in the files; what I hadn't anticipated was the effect just seeing them would have on me. That period of my life sometimes seemed like a nightmare, but now that I'd taken possession of the truth that was contained in those boxes, there was no escaping the fact that it had been real. Some people who want to know about their childhood can ask their parents and look at photograph albums. The only record of my childhood was in the files I'd just obtained by making an official request to social services.

I will always be immensely grateful to Pam for her friendship and for taking me in when I needed somewhere to go where I could feel safe and wouldn't be alone while I read what had been written about my past. Because the records officer had been right and some of things I discovered were very difficult to come to terms with. I hadn't known, for example, that my teachers were aware that I was being sold and trafficked; that before he told me not to contact him again, my brother Ben told social services he was concerned for my safety at Denver House; that my dad had been told I was choosing to have sex with 'adult Asian males'; that a friend of my mum's had reported to social services a conversation they'd had during which Mum said I needed to be put away in an institution and she wished I wasn't her daughter; that my nan had written a letter to social services saying there was something wrong with me mentally; that my social worker thought she knew the man who was taking me to Birmingham and that he worked for the prison service; that although I was told I *had* to leave Highfield when I turned 18 – even though it was reported that I wasn't ready to live independently – social services could have continued to accommodate me until I was 21, but funding was denied; that despite what my leaving care worker told me about younger children needing her attention and that I should take responsibility for myself now that I was 18, it was my right to ask her for help until I was 21.

What I also read in my files was that my nan went to Denver House several times while I was living there to tell the staff that I was mentally ill and they shouldn't take any notice of anything I said. She had plenty to say at the meeting she forced her way into too. According to the notes, one of the things that was discussed at that meeting was the fact that I had recently told a member of staff that the men who were trafficking me had started taking me to houses in Birmingham, which was about an hour's drive away on the motorway from the town we lived in. Nan didn't want to know about any of that, however. She hadn't come to hear about my problems. She'd come to tell the social worker and everyone else who was at the meeting, 'You do know Zoe tells lies, don't you? She's not well. She needs help.' Which made some sort of sense now that I knew about what Granddad had done to Mum when she was a little girl, and possibly to me too: Nan must have been very anxious for everyone to believe I was a liar, that nothing I said should be trusted, and that I was solely to blame for anything that had *ever* happened to me.

There were a lot of things in the files that shocked and upset me, amongst the worst of which were some of the notes I used to leave in my room with pathetic pleas for help and details of addresses, phone and car registration numbers so that they might know where to start looking for me 'if I don't come back'. When I found those notes in the files, it was almost as if they related to some other little girl, and I sobbed as I read the words I'd scrawled hastily on them all those years ago, because I knew then that the staff had read them too, and still had done nothing to try to help me.

As I worked my way through page after page of notes and records, I finally began to understand just how badly I'd been let down. In fact, the only person who really seemed to have cared about what happened to me was Mandy, the nice woman from the NSPCC, who had written a letter to social services saying, in effect, that I was no safer at Denver House than I had been with my mum and dad, that if the situation at the unit had occurred in a family home, the child involved would have been removed instantly, and that she couldn't understand why it was being allowed to happen. And even then, nobody did anything.

One thing that struck me as peculiar as I worked my way through the files was that there was no record of anything that had happened during the last three months I was in Denver House. Everything else was there, filed in date order, including all the daily record sheets that had to be filled in by staff at the unit, which attested to meals I hadn't eaten, baths I hadn't had and hot drinks I hadn't drunk every night before I went to bed. It was just those last three months that were missing, which were the worst months of all. In fact, the last entry in the files is a note that says, 'Zoe is doing a lot better now. She's not going to Birmingham anymore.' But that wasn't true. The trafficking never stopped the whole time I was there, and I certainly never told anyone that it had.

Something else that was missing from my files was any mention of the meeting I'd had with Frances's boss when I was living at Highfield, after Frances had asked me to babysit overnight for her little boy. It was a formal meeting – with another woman taking minutes – which I realised later had been held because her boss was concerned about our relationship. And although those specific concerns were unfounded, it did seem strange that there wasn't any record of what was actually very inappropriate behaviour by a member of staff. I don't know why anyone would bother to remove any mention of it, however, when there was so much other evidence of the fact that no one ever did anything to stop the sexual abuse and trafficking they *knew* were going on, or tried to make life more bearable for a young teenage girl who kept pleading for their help.

Looking back at that horrific period of my life from a different perspective finally allowed me to see it clearly, and I think it was the first time I'd ever really understood that what had happened to me was wrong. I'd never felt safe at home, but I thought I would *feel* safe and *be* safe when I was taken into care. It wasn't as though there was some reason why they couldn't take care of me properly: I wasn't doing any of it willing, and it wouldn't have required much effort on behalf of my social worker and the staff at the unit to protect me. I still don't understand why they didn't do it – for me and for all the other children they must have let down equally badly in various ways. That was perhaps the most difficult aspect of it all – realising that everything could have been so easily prevented.

That's what Pam thought, too, when she read my files. 'I think you deserve an apology for the total lack of care you received,' she told me. 'If you want, I can try and find a solicitor who could look at the evidence and see if you've got a case.'

We talked about it quite a lot before I asked her to go ahead. I didn't really think it would come to anything, but once the idea had taken root, I became almost obsessed by the thought that someone might actually say they were sorry and take responsibility for all the things they'd allowed to happen to me.

Staying in the room at Pam's house was only going to be a temporary measure, so I'd kept on the flat I'd lived in for almost the last ten years. Eventually though, when I got a letter from the council saying they'd been informed that I wasn't living there anymore, I was forced to make a decision. Was I going to return to live alone in the flat that was the only place I'd ever known as mine, in the town where I'd grown up and suffered horrific abuse, but where, despite everything, I felt I belonged? Or was I going to move to the town where Pam lived and where she was happy to offer me a room for as long as I needed it? It was a surprisingly difficult decision to make. In the end, I let the flat go, by which time Pam had found me a solicitor.

Chapter 20

Leaving my home town meant that I'd be walking away from any possibility there might have been that my mum would ever be any different. I don't know why I'd clung for so long to the hope that one day she might say she was sorry for the way she'd always treated me and that she realised she did love me after all. I suppose I'd always known deep down that it wasn't ever going to happen, but it was an incredibly difficult truth to accept.

What also made me very anxious about giving up the flat and moving was that there were no certainties involved. I didn't have a job, and although Pam had already done a great deal to help me – more than any member of my own family had ever done – without ever asking for or expecting anything in return, I was still too afraid to trust anyone. So I knew I could easily end up in the same situation I'd been in before, only this time in a town I didn't know. As things turned out, however, it was probably the best decision I've ever made.

I quite honestly don't know if I'd still be here today if I hadn't met Pam when I did. She helped me through a lot at that time, and she's still there for me today – sometimes as my best friend and sometimes more like the mother I never had. It was as if our meeting was meant to be, for me at least. So I was very relieved when she offered to go with me to London to see the solicitor who'd agreed to look at my case.

The solicitor's name was Shamra and she worked with a firm that specialises in serious cases of medical negligence and child abuse. It was quite a trek from the train station to her office lugging the heavy suitcase that contained all my files, and I was very nervous about meeting her. But she turned out to be really nice. So I left the files with her and went back with Pam to her house, where I tried to live as normal a life as possible while I waited for Shamra to read them.

When the phone call from Shamra finally came, she told me she *would* take on my case, then added, 'I feel really confident we can win.'

I knew there was a long way to go before anything actually happened, and that there were no guarantees. But the fact that an experienced solicitor like Shamra thought I had a case was a vindication in itself, and another step in the process of accepting the fact that it hadn't all been my fault.

After the news had sunk in, I managed to contact Debbie – the girl at Denver House who had also been bullied and trafficked by Natalie – to explain what had happened and ask her if she wanted to be included.

'I got my records from social services too,' she told me when we spoke on the phone. 'But much as I'd like to be involved, I couldn't face reliving all those horrendous memories.'

'I understand,' I answered. 'I'm really anxious about that too. But I think, for me, the need to have someone accept responsibility for what happened and say they're sorry so that maybe I won't feel so angry about it anymore almost outweighs the fear of what's going to be involved.'

Then we talked about other things for a few minutes, before Debbie said, 'You know, I do have some happy memories of Denver House, of those evenings we got away from everything and shared a bottle of cider.'

'I feel the same,' I told her. 'It makes you realise how important it is to have a friend.'

Meanwhile, the solicitor arranged for my files to be reviewed by an expert social worker, who concluded that I had done more to try to keep myself safe than any of the people who were put in charge of my care had ever done. It made me feel a bit better when he said that, because it was confirmation of the fact that I *did* try to help myself but that there was very little a frightened, intimidated teenager could do when none of the staff at the children's homes, none of the social workers and none of the police officers I ever pleaded with for help did anything at all to protect me.

On my second visit to London for a meeting with the solicitor, Shamra arranged for me to see a psychiatrist, who said I've got post-traumatic stress disorder (PTSD) and something called emotionally unstable personality disorder, which is apparently characterised by an unstable sense of self, unstable emotions and unstable relationships with other people – which I suppose pretty much sums it up.

After the psychiatrist had written a report, the solicitor put together the evidence for my case and sent it all to the council's solicitor. It was a long and complicated process that took almost two years, during which time I continued to live at Pam's house. I was claiming benefits and felt as though I was living in limbo, just waiting for whatever was going to happen next, and I was really glad not to be on my own.

It was during that waiting period that Pam gave me some driving lessons for my birthday. I burst into tears when she told me, because I'd always wanted to learn to drive but thought I was too stupid. So I was very proud when I picked it up really quickly and was able to drive home to Pam's house at the end of my first lesson. Six months later, I took my test and, much to my surprise, passed first time. I had been told all my life that I was nothing, I was thick, there was something wrong with me, I wouldn't ever be able to do the sort of things normal people do … And I'd believed it.

Before I went to live at Denver House, Mum used to joke about my lack of confidence, the fact that I found it difficult to look people in the eye, that I only spoke if I was spoken to, and that I was too timid to go anywhere on my own. In fact, I can remember Ben saying one day that if I ever dared to go on a bus alone, I would have to walk on to it backwards to avoid making eye contact with the driver. Then he and Mum roared with laughter.

Now though, I had a driving licence to prove that I was more competent than I'd thought I was!

The case that Shamra put together on my behalf was for damages for 'personal and psychiatric injuries and consequential losses arising from sexual, physical and emotional abuse suffered as a result of social services' negligence' when I was between 13 and 21 years old. Amongst the vast piles of papers and documents, there was something else Shamra wrote that made me feel quite emotional, but that I thought summed up the case very succinctly: 'Hers is a very sad story, with so many missed opportunities by family members, social workers and the police to step in and rescue her. She is a very intelligent young woman who could have pursued a career and lived a very "normal" life but was deprived of this opportunity from a very young age.'

Eventually, the council responded, although not until just before the legal deadline, and I'm pretty certain that sympathy for me didn't play any part in their decision not to offer any defence and to want to settle out of court. So then there was a settlement meeting in London, which again Pam came to with me.

The council's solicitor and barrister were in one room, while Pam and I, a barrister, my solicitor and another woman from the firm were in a different one, although Shamra and our barrister spent most of the day going back and forth between the two, making offers and being given counter-offers until eventually a sum was agreed on.

When Pam and I left and were heading back to the train station, I decided to treat us to some cake. There was a Morrisons supermarket on the corner just opposite the station and when we walked in, they were playing a Céline Dion song called 'Incredible' and I can remember thinking, 'Yes! Love *is* incredible. It's what I've held on to throughout all these years, and it's what motivates people like Pam and Shamra to do the things they do for other people.' So it seemed very fitting that we should have chosen that moment on that day to walk into that supermarket.

I know some people have nothing good to say about lawyers, but my solicitor was brilliant. I had plenty of experience while I was at Denver House and subsequently of people who were just doing a job and didn't really care about the person on the receiving end. So I know that Shamra *did* care – about me and about ensuring that the council accepted the fact that they'd made mistakes so that, hopefully, they wouldn't make the same ones again.

Although I would have hated to have had to go into a courtroom where I might have been bullied, disbelieved and disparaged by the council's barrister, I would have liked some answers to the many questions I still have about why it was all allowed to happen. But I suppose it was because they didn't *have* any answers to those questions that the council was so anxious to settle out of court.

I also sometimes wonder what action, if any, the council took against the members of staff who failed so abysmally to provide even a small part of 'what is necessary for the health, welfare, maintenance, and protection' of the children in their care. I know that some of the people who worked at Denver House while I was there still work for the same council, although not all of them in social services. In fact, I saw a TV documentary not long ago with a bit in it that involved a woman who was a member of staff when I was there. She was doing a completely different job, but she was still the same bossy, aggressive woman who punched me in the face and cut my lip when she was restraining me one day by pinning me down on the floor because I'd refused to give up the bottle of beer she found me drinking. She was being given verbal abuse by a member of the public in the TV programme, which made me laugh because he clearly didn't know who he was dealing with!

The settlement that was reached was quite a lot of money in terms of what I'd been earning at the warehouse and as a fitness trainer, and Shamra said it set a precedent for similar cases, which I was pleased about, because it meant that it might help other people get a bit more in the future too. So it was a good outcome in that respect, particularly as I hadn't really expected to get anything at all. But it was a hollow victory in some ways, because it seemed to highlight the fact that no amount of money can ever erase what happened to me, repair the damage that's been done to me, or heal the many psychological and emotional wounds I've been left with, which I know will continue to affect me to some degree for the rest of my life.

One of the positive aspects of receiving the money was that it enabled me to buy a car and a little house in a town about ten miles away from where Pam lives. I got the house for quite a good price because it needs some doing up, and it really does make a difference to me psychologically to know that I'm safe and don't have to depend on anyone else. I think Pam must have heaved a sigh of relief too, when I finally moved all my stuff out of her house!

I haven't lived in my own place for very long. I found it difficult to relax when I first moved in, and was still scared to go to bed at night. The warnings my mum used to give me about hands in my bed, and the stories she used to tell me about my dad still affect my sleep even today; I think they always will. So I'd drink every evening to begin with, which did make me a bit less frightened, but didn't stop the horrible nightmares I've had to accept I'll also probably always have. Then, one day, I thought to myself, 'I didn't ever believe I would escape, but I have. I got out. And now this is going to be my home. I can't change the past. I can't get back what I've lost. But I can put all my efforts into making a better future for myself. I've done it once and I can do it again. I deserve to feel safe and to be able to enjoy my life.'

They say that what doesn't kill you makes you stronger. Well, maybe I'd been strong all along without realising it; I just wasn't strong enough as a child to cope with being ill-treated and abandoned by my parents, let down by social services, and trafficked by men who didn't really see me and the other girls they were exploiting as being human beings like they were.

I still feel that I've been robbed – of a childhood and of the chance to live a normal life – and I sometimes feel very sad when I think about everything I've lost. But I know I'm lucky too, because there are things I want to do now that give me a reason to get up in the mornings. And for the first time in my life I can actually imagine having a future and growing old.

When everything's stripped away and all you're left with is you, there has to be something positive inside you that makes you believe it's worth carrying on. Whatever that something is, I've been surprised to find that I've got it inside me. Maybe that's why, when I used to feel angry with myself for not being able to give up properly, something always seemed to cushion my fall just before I hit rock bottom.

One day, after I'd moved into my own house, I decided to write down three different questions – Will I find my soulmate? Will I be okay? Will I ever be happy? – and put one under my pillow every night for the next three nights, in the hope that I might get answers to them in my dreams. Nothing happened on the first or second night, but on the third I had a bizarre dream about my dad. He was wearing the work clothes he always wore when I was a little girl and used to wave to him as he was going to work, and he was very emotional because he knew he was dead and couldn't stay with me. Then he started singing a Westlife song called 'Angel's Wings', which I hadn't ever heard him sing when he was alive.

The words of the song were still going round in my head when I woke up, particularly the bit about knowing that, whatever the question, love is the answer. Suddenly I realised that the love I'd been searching for wasn't the sort of love I'd hoped to share with Jess. It was much bigger than that, because what really matters is having the ability to love and care about other people, rather than expecting to *be* loved. I'd been so fixated on one day finding someone special, I hadn't realised I'd already got special people in my life – Tony and his mum Evelyn, who still keeps in touch with me; Shamra, who believed in me and helped me fight for justice; and Pam, who I know will always look out for me and be there when I need help.

It was like a release, letting go of the sense of failure I'd felt because I hadn't found the partner I'd always thought was out there somewhere waiting for me. What I should have realised after my disastrous relationship with Jess was that that sort of love doesn't *belong* to you, the way the other sort does. I'd put everything into that relationship, but what I was really trying to do was fill the empty space inside *me*, the space where my mother's love should have been. I think that's what Jess was trying to do too, which meant that our relationship was built on need rather than love. And maybe any relationship between two needy people who aren't able to fulfil the need in each other is bound to fail.

Chapter 21

I haven't seen my mum for more than a year now. The reason I always clung to the hope that I could fix things for her and with her was because I thought it was my fault that she didn't love me. Reading my social services files and winning my case made me re-evaluate that belief, and when I realised it hadn't ever been my fault, I also had to accept the fact that I couldn't fix it. Only she can do that, although first she'd have to take responsibility for what she did, and I don't think that will ever happen.

It's really hard to say this, but I think she hates me and always has done. What's even more difficult to come to terms with is the way she deliberately turned me against my dad by telling me lies about him and making me afraid of him, simply because she didn't want me to have a good relationship with *my* dad when she hadn't had one with *hers*.

She must have had a horrible childhood. But the irony is that the reason I can sympathise and understand what that must have been like is because I had a horrible childhood too – thanks entirely to her. Because although social services were responsible for a lot of the terrible things that happened to me, it was because of what my mum did that I was taken into care in the first place, although she blames me for *that* as well.

I do feel sorry for her sometimes, because I think I've got something at the core of me that she hasn't got – something that allows me to see things in a different perspective and that nothing can reach, however bad things become. I'm not consciously aware of it all the time, just often enough to keep me moving forward in my life, despite the occasions when everything seems to unravel and I find myself almost back where I started, with another huge struggle ahead of me.

I stopped seeing my nan about three years ago too. I went to her house to clean it, wash her clothes and cook her a hot meal every day for several months. But even when Nan was reliant on me for her day-to-day care, she criticised everything I did – I couldn't cook as well as her, I didn't make the fire as well as she did, I wasn't as good at cleaning up as she was ...

Mum did her shopping once a week and dropped it off at her door, and although Ben visited her occasionally, Jake and Michael never did. In fact, none of us saw much of Michael after Dad died. They'd had a good relationship and Michael took his death really badly, which resulted in him going off the rails a bit and spending most of his time at friends' houses.

Then Nan went to live in a home, and after visiting her there a few times and having to listen to her making spiteful comments about me, I stopped going the day she said, 'Your brothers must be very ashamed to have a sister like you.' She was referring to my sexuality, because I was living with Jess at the time. But it made me think about the fact that she had never liked me, never said anything nice *to* me or *about* me, and never tried to do anything *for* me. So I decided, 'You know what? I don't need this anymore.'

After Mum told me that she'd been abused by her dad when she was a little girl, I didn't talk to anyone about it until eight years ago, when I told Ben about some of it. We didn't really discuss it; I just remember being surprised that he didn't seem to be particularly shocked by it. But I think he's struggling with it now, because of the things Nan said before she died a few months ago.

Nan had always been a bit of a snob and was very concerned about what other people might think. In fact, according to Mum, Nan had only married Granddad because she was pregnant with her. What Mum also told me after Dad died was that Nan had been quite happy for her to have a relationship with an older, married man when she was in her late teens and still living at home, simply because he had an expensive car that he used to park outside their house, where all the neighbours could see it. And apparently, from what Ben told me later, right up to the moment she died, Nan was still blaming Mum for what Granddad did to her when she was a little girl. In fact, all she seemed to be concerned about was Mum continuing to keep the secret.

I wasn't there when Nan died. No one told me how ill she was, not even Ben, which I found very hurtful. Ben and Mum were with her just before she passed away though, and Ben said she kept saying, 'I'll never tell. It was terrible,' then looking frightened, as if she could see something no one else could see.

'What was terrible, Nan?' Ben said he asked her. 'What did you see?'

'I didn't *see* it. I heard it,' she whispered. Then, a bit later, after she seemed to have calmed down again, she suddenly said, 'It was sexual though. I know it was,' before adding angrily, 'But *she* was always showing her Mary off.' And then, 'I'm ready now. I'm ready for God.'

She'd been in a home for five or six years by that time and she used to do things like refusing to wash or go to the toilet. But she didn't have dementia; she was just being stubborn for some reason. Then she got ill and was taken to hospital, and after a couple of days they said there was nothing more they could do because her organs were shutting down. So they all knew she was going to die, and still no one bothered to tell me, which, in retrospect, was probably a good thing, because I'm sure that if I had gone to see her, she'd only have said something nasty to me; and if I'd known she was dying and hadn't gone, I'd have felt guilty.

When Ben told me later what she'd been saying, I realised that until the moment she died her only concern was what it always had been – to protect herself against any accusation that she'd been to blame for doing nothing to stop her husband sexually abusing their daughter. She let it happen and then made Mum keep it a secret; not because she was sorry for the role she'd played, but because it wasn't the sort of thing she wanted other people to know about.

'Mum went to see her every day when she was in hospital,' Ben told me, 'and on the last day, when Nan knew she was dying and Mum had gone there straight from work, all Nan said to her was, "Did you have to come dressed like that?"'

Apparently, her last words were 'It was terrible.'

Mum rang to let me know that Nan had died. But I didn't go to the funeral. When she phoned again not long afterwards, she talked a lot about Nan and about how it had been her fault Mum hasn't been the woman she should have been. And because she was nice to me during the phone call, I thought maybe she was starting to work things through in her mind and might eventually realise that I hadn't actually been to blame for her unhappiness. Then she phoned again a couple of days later to say, 'I'm cutting you out of my will. Why should I leave anything to you when you've done nothing to help me? You're dead to me now.'

I shouldn't have been hurt by it after all the cruel things she's said and done to me for as long as I can remember. But I was. Apparently though, I'm not the only one of her children she's cutting out of her will: Ben told me she's going to leave the house to him, which is the only thing she has. It needs a lot of work, and Ben was telling me about all the improvements he's going to make to it – not now, while she's alive and could benefit from them, but after she's dead. He didn't seem to see any irony in what he was saying. But perhaps there's some sort of karmic justice in it all, because she was very opposed to Dad buying the house when he did, and when he died and she discovered he'd paid off the mortgage and it belonged to her, she just laughed and said, 'I win.'

I know she's in a world of her own and doesn't have any comprehension of what she's done – to all her children, in one way or another. But I really thought that what my nan said just before she died might open her eyes and make her start to think about it. Because I *do* love her, despite everything. Then I began to realise that all her long phone calls to me, when she talked about how upset she'd been by things her mum had said to her, were supposed to make me feel sorry for her. So although I tried to be sympathetic, I kept thinking, 'Am I missing something here? Can she really not make the connection between what her own mother said and did and what she's done – and continues to do – herself?' Obviously, the answer was 'No'.

I did my fourth detox a few months ago, which this time, rather than being home medicated, was a seven-day programme that involved spending a few hours every day for the first three days at an alcohol recovery centre and taking a drug to minimise withdrawal symptoms and anxiety and help me sleep. I imagine a lot of people must think, 'Why don't you just stop drinking? You know it's ruining your life and preventing you from doing things that might make you happy. So just stop.' Unfortunately, however, it isn't as easy as that: if it was, believe me, I'd have done it and stuck to it a long time ago.

When I'd completed the programme, I started boxing training again, and doing daily workouts that include running, weight training, bodyweight exercises and yoga, plus training three times a week at the boxing gym, where I've had a tremendous amount of support and encouragement from all the coaches. I was determined to get back to where I'd been before I met Jess, and just a few weeks ago I was told I'm going to get my boxing licence and that, as well as being able to fight as an amateur boxer for the club – as soon as I've shifted the last few pounds of extra weight – they're going to pay for me to train as a boxing coach so that I can work alongside them to help other people the way they've helped me.

I want this opportunity more than I've ever wanted anything. Before I started boxing, I didn't really know what it felt like to set myself a goal and make it happen. So maybe, once I've achieved this, I'll find that there are other things I want to do and I'll make them happen too.

For now, I'm taking it one day at a time, focusing on getting fit again and on my recovery from post-traumatic stress and alcohol dependence. As well as attending support groups for people with alcohol problems and for survivors of sexual abuse whenever I need them, I'm about to start weekly trauma counselling. I also listen to guided meditation on my headphones every night, which helps me to relax and go to sleep as well as keeping me grounded and focused. I find it helpful to say positive affirmations in front of the mirror every morning too. Then I take my dog for a walk.

I got my dog when she was a puppy and she has been responsible for some of the most dramatic changes in my life, by helping me to overcome my fear of leaving the house, and by always being there whenever I wake up from a horrible nightmare or have a flashback or intrusive thought. It was because of her that I've recently had another opportunity too, to assist a dog trainer with some of the classes I take *my* dog to.

I've got a meditation space in my house where I keep quotes and other items that mean something to me – books and my yoga mat, for example – and there's one quote I really like, which is from an American writer called Andre Dubus, who had some horrible traumatic experiences:

We receive and we lose, and we must try to achieve
gratitude; and with that gratitude to embrace with
whole hearts whatever of life that remains after the
losses.

I think the reason it resonates with me is because, as well
as seeming to shine a light on my own situation, it reminds
me that that's what I have to do – be grateful for what I
have, for the things I didn't lose, and try to move on.
Having deliberately set out to ruin my childhood, my
mum must have succeeded way beyond her wildest expec-
tations. But I know now that I can either keep looking
over my shoulder for the rest of my life or I can decide to
make a future for myself based on my own values and
aspirations.

When I first went to see the solicitor to find out if I had
grounds for a case against social services, I had already
been assessed several times and found to be unfit for work
and was dependent on the Employment and Support
Allowance I was receiving. So I was really anxious about
the future, because I knew I couldn't live at Pam's place
forever and that I was eventually going to have to find
another miserable flat I wouldn't be able to afford to heat.

When my dad died in his late sixties, he was already
showing signs of dementia, and I was also really scared
that if I lived long enough, I might get it too, then I'd be
put in another kind of care home, which is something I
can't even bear to think about.

I know that many of the fears and anxieties that were instilled in me as a child, first by my mother and then at Denver House, will always be there – the problems I have socialising; my distrust of other people; the sense of self-disgust I experience if I ever have any sexual urges; my fear of physical contact, which means that even when I'm distressed and want to be comforted, I can't bear anyone to come near. But I think I will be able to live with those anxieties now that I'm finally free to be who I want to be. And that's a good feeling, as well as a completely new experience for me. I don't know what lies ahead, but I do know that it wouldn't make any sense to give up now, when the hardest part is already behind me.

It turns out that love really was the answer all along – not romantic love, as I'd thought, but being able to love life, nature, other people and myself, so that I can forgive myself for the mistakes I've made. For the first 27 years of my life, before I met Pam, no one cared about me. But now *I* care, and although I know I'm going to need quite a lot of help, I'm ready to take responsibility for my own 'health, welfare, maintenance, and protection', and to pay 'serious attention to avoid any [further] damage or risk', so that, finally, I can have the life I deserve.

About the Authors

Practise what you love with love, working IN the moment and not FOR a moment. The world does not stop for defeat or for victory and neither should you.

Zoe Patterson wrote the note above after completing her first half marathon. She realised she'd spent so much time focusing on the end goal, rather than enjoying the process of training and seeing herself improve, that she had nothing left to focus on when the race was over. That's when she knew she had to follow her heart and do what she loved doing, which is when she started boxing.

Zoe knows from her own experiences that by doing what you love simply because you love doing it, you can transform your life, even save it. It may not make you rich or famous, but it *will* make you happy – which, for many years, was something Zoe didn't believe she would ever be. Now, through her work as a personal trainer and boxing coach – and via the blog she has recently started at zoepattersonfightingback.com – she is finally achieving her dream of passing on what she has learned to other people who are struggling to find a way of fighting back.

Jane Smith is the ghostwriter of numerous best-selling books, including several *Sunday Times* top ten bestsellers: www.janesmithghostwriter.com

eNewsletter

Moving Memoirs

Stories of hope, courage and the power of love…

If you loved this book, then you will love our Moving Memoirs eNewsletter

Sign up to…

- Be the first to hear about new books
- Get sneak previews from your favourite authors
- Read exclusive interviews
- Be entered into our monthly prize draw to win one of our latest releases before it's even hit the shops!

Sign up at

www.moving-memoirs.com